Paradise Delayed

The pitfalls and pleasures (mainly the pitfalls) of Caribbean island life in the beautiful archipelago of Bocas del Toro, Panama

by

Ian Usher

Paradise Delayed

Ian Usher

Copyright © 2013 by Ian Usher

Cover art copyright © 2013 by Ian Usher

Published by Wider Vision Publishing

www.WiderVisionPublishing.com

Contents

Introduction	1
Prologue	2
How to buy a Caribbean island	4
Boat handling for dummies	7
Log jam	10
Language barriers	12
Chainsaw challenges	16
Engine issues	19
"There's water coming in at the front!"	24
House roof underwater	29
Lost in the mangroves	37
Baby birds	41
Border crossings	44
Cameron's trip home	53
The Bocas Net	60
Oven relocation	65
Maxie's medicine	70
A Caribbean Christmas	73
Kent's boat	75
Secret lagoon	87
Big Red bites the dust	92
Jungle wedding fever	103
Epilogue	105
Acknowledgements	107
About the author	109

Note: For book extras, including photos illustrating each chapter, and some video clips too, please go to:-
ParadiseDelayed.com

Introduction

In 2008, two years after an unplanned, unfortunate and traumatic detour off the anticipated trajectory of my life, I decided that it was time for a change. I wanted to leave a painful past behind and make a new start.

Little did I know that the new life I went looking for would ultimately lead me to ownership of a Caribbean island. It sounds like a dream come true, doesn't it? In many ways it is, but there are certainly plenty of challenges too.

I bought my island in 2011, immediately beginning my ascent of an almost vertical learning curve. As is often the case, the experiences that seem so difficult and challenging at the time are ultimately the ones that become the favourite stories, recounted again and again for the amusement of others.

These tales in no way provide a balanced view of life on a Caribbean island, as most involve some kind of problem, difficulty, or challenge.

But tales of sitting in a hammock reading a book just don't make for compelling reading, do they?

Prologue

In 2010 I had come to the end of one of the most incredible adventures of my life. Having put my "whole life" up for sale on eBay in 2008, following a painful divorce, I found myself wondering what I wanted to do next. There had been a great deal of worldwide publicity about my life-selling adventure, and I had been asked many times in interviews what I would do once I had sold my life. My usual glib response had always been, "Anything I like, really."

I too had asked myself many times what I really wanted to do next, and I had made lists - lots of them. These were ultimately distilled into a list of 100 lifetime goals - places I wanted to see, things I wanted to do, people I wanted to meet - and I set myself the challenge to achieve them all in a period of 100 weeks.

My two-year journey, during which I completed 93 of the 100 goals I had set for myself, ended on 4th July 2010, in the crown of the Statue of Liberty in New York. Very appropriate, I thought, as Lady Liberty has been such a symbol of new beginnings for so many for so long. I was heading to Whitehorse to make a fresh start with a new partner in my life.

I had met Moe in December 2008 in Whitehorse in Canada's chilly Yukon Territory while achieving my goal to run a dog sled team in the wilderness. We had enjoyed a brief romance, but hadn't seen each other for the next fifteen months, as my globetrotting adventures had continued.

We had kept in touch and eventually managed to arrange to meet again in April 2010. We spent more time together in Florida, Jamaica, and Costa Rica - a big change from the last time we had shared in the dark December days in the frozen north.

We both enjoyed our tropical vacation, and re-kindled our relationship. In July that year, at the end of my journey, I was heading back to Whitehorse to start a new life with Moe, and her two kids Finn and Maible.

Life was wonderful there in the summer, but towards Christmas temperatures fell to around 30 below (degrees Celsius!!). In a wooden cabin in the forest this was just a bit too cold for my liking.

I somewhat randomly came across an article entitled *"The World's Ten Cheapest Tropical Places to Live"*. A couple of places really took my fancy, and in early 2011 Moe and I took a trip back to the Caribbean to take a look at property possibilities in Panama.

Prologue

The trip ultimately ended in ownership of my own Caribbean island. In August 2011, after a second summer in Whitehorse, I again headed for warmer Caribbean weather, this time with a property to sort out when I got there.

When I first arrived in Bocas del Toro to begin work on the property I had nowhere to stay, but through a couple of lucky contacts I was invited to house-sit a beautiful property at the north end of the Isla Colon. I stayed there for three wonderful weeks. On week days I would use the owners' car to commute into town to meet my workers, and then travel by boat to my island to do a full day's work. On weekends I had little to do but read, play with the dogs I was looking after, or snorkel from the little private beach. It was the Caribbean dream come true.

I met a few of the neighbours and was invited to a Sunday gathering. Over a couple of beers I quizzed one of my new friends about the challenges of building a house in such a place. There seemed to be so many things I didn't know, and so many challenges to overcome.

"What we need is a book that addresses all of those issues," I suggested.

Kitty looked at me in horror. "No we don't!" she said. "We've had to go through the same challenges, and I think it's a bit of a sorting process. Many people only last a couple of months before they give up and go back home. You have to be tougher than that to make it here. You have to earn it. If people can't manage without a *Panama Homes for Dummies* guidebook, I don't really want them as my neighbours."

I loved her attitude, and her little pep talk just hardened my resolve to be one of those who did earn the right to be here. A couple of years later I find that I now understand and agree with Kitty whole-heartedly. If you are looking for a *Panama How-To* book, I'm afraid this isn't it.

This is a gathering of true tales relating some of some of my experiences since I arrived in this beautiful, but challenging, place.

I hope you enjoy my little slice of "paradise"!

How to buy a Caribbean island

We stepped off the boat carefully, hoping not to fall through the rotting planks on the dilapidated dock. This was to be the last property that we would view that day, and in true real estate agent fashion, Mark had saved what appeared to be the best until last.

Moe and I had arrived in Panama a couple of weeks earlier. We had travelled along the Pacific coast looking at several property hotspot locations, but nothing had really inspired us. In Panama City we were more like tourists than property hunters, and enjoyed seeing the Panama Canal.

I was really looking forward to getting to the small archipelago of Bocas del Toro on the Caribbean coast, because that was where we planned to invest most of our property research efforts. We weren't disappointed.

Bocas Town is a tropically colourful place, more akin to Jamaica than anything else we had seen in Panama, and we loved the place at once. We spent a few days in town, and looked at properties in the surrounding countryside. But it was the islands we had really come to see.

We had arranged to be shown around by Mark, a friendly guy from Alabama. After many years working in the Florida real estate industry he had made the move down to the Caribbean and taken over a small real estate business in Bocas.

The last property on the list for today was a two acre island, about twenty minutes by boat to the south of the main town. The place had been owned for several years by an English guy, Mark informed us, who was very keen to sell. The owner hadn't been around for some time, and the island had become very overgrown. The wooden dock had fallen into disrepair, and some of the planks were beginning to rot. We carefully made our way along the dock from the boat, setting foot on land at the far end.

We could only see for a few metres, as the trees and bushes were quite thick, and we tried to penetrate a little further to get an idea of the size and shape of the property. It looked promising, but obviously needed much work.

On the boat ride back to town Mark told us more about the island and the current owner, suggesting that he may be open to an offer, should we care to make one.

That evening Moe and I studied maps and discussed the properties we had seen. Moe was keen on some of the larger properties we had seen, many of which had more than enough acreage for horses, one of her passions. But my interest kept returning to the last property we had seen that day - the mysterious island, much of which we hadn't been able to see.

As Moe already owned a property up in Whitehorse, it was going to be my purchase alone down here in Panama. We decided that we needed to take a more thorough look at the island. We called Mark the next morning and arranged to return that afternoon, hoping to penetrate further into the property.

Dressed in more appropriately sturdy footwear and clothing, we managed to battle our way around the edge of the island, completing a full circumnavigation, eventually arriving back at the dock. The island was low-lying, but drier than many of the other properties we had seen. It had a couple of slightly clearer areas where we could get a bit of a view into the centre too.

There were three docks, the current owner having considered splitting the property into three separate blocks and selling them individually, Mark explained. However, since the downturn in the US economy in 2008, property values in Panama had been affected, and the owner hadn't managed to make a sale.

"He should clear the place a bit," I suggested. "It would be much easier to sell if you could actually see some of the island."

"That's what I've told him," Mark answered. "He's not willing, or perhaps not able to spend another cent on the place. He really is keen to sell." Mark again suggested that it could be worth making an offer if we really were interested in the place.

"What sort of offer might tempt him?" I asked, fishing for information.

"Ah, I can't be both the buyer and seller," Mark laughed, but did tell me that the owner had previously been made a very low offer, which he had rejected. Apparently he now wished he had accepted.

With some kind of idea of a price that might be acceptable, that evening Moe and I again discussed possibilities further. I think Moe was as excited as I was, but tried to temper my enthusiasm. I could only see positives, by far the largest of which was that it was a whole Caribbean island! A whole island which, apparently, could be bought at a price well below anything I could have possibly imagined.

Paradise Delayed

"Our own private Caribbean island," I kept repeating to Moe, I imagine with a big grin on my face. "I'm going to make a ridiculous offer."

It turned out that my offer wasn't as ridiculous as I had initially thought. Mark put it forward to the owner, and that evening, over dinner, said that the owner had come back with a counter-offer. It was only a couple of thousand above what I had initially offered, and with Moe enthusiastically kicking my shin under the table, we agreed on a price.

The next day, at Mark's office, he grinned as we all sat down. "Congratulations!" he beamed. "Looks like you are the owner of a Caribbean island."

This was only supposed to be a fact-finding trip, I thought to myself, but my impulsive nature seemed to have asserted itself as usual. I had no idea what I was going to do next, but I was grinning foolishly. "We own a Caribbean island!" I said to Moe, and we both laughed.

Of course, nothing is certain until all the paperwork is complete and money changes hands. After studying the paperwork he had on the property, we left a deposit with Mark. He put us in touch with a local attorney, who turned out to be very efficient. She was already on the case for us by the time we got back to Whitehorse a few days later.

With only a few minor hiccups in transferring funds from my Australian bank account to the attorney in Panama, all formalities were completed within a couple of months. It was official - we were now owners of our own (extremely overgrown) private Caribbean island.

Boat handling for dummies

When I returned to Panama to start work on the island one of the first purchases I had to make was a boat. I needed to be able to get from town to the property and back, and be able to take workers to help with clearing the thick jungle, which had reclaimed much of the island during the previous years of neglect.

I really didn't know very much about boats, but did have some experience with two stroke engines, from owning both motorbikes and jet skis. At least I had some sort of idea what a decent engine should sound like.

As I wandered the town, I would ask anyone that I met, local and gringo alike, if they knew of anyone who had a boat for sale. Over the course of a week or so I was shown many possibilities - it seemed that almost everyone knew someone who had a boat, which they might sell for the right price.

Many of the prices I was quoted seemed ridiculously high, and I think many of the potential sellers, mainly locals, were just trying their luck, hoping they had found a rich gringo who would buy the first boat he was offered.

I soon got a good idea of values, and stumbled across a boat that was pulled up into storage, on the grass at the local marina. Three people had told me about this boat, and I had three different possible prices. Finally, one of my contacts gave me the phone number of the owner and suggested I deal direct with him.

The owner wasn't in town for a few days, but he said I could take the boat out to try out the engine if I wished. By asking around at one of the hostels I managed to round up a couple of burly local guys, including one familiar with boats and engines. We took a water taxi over to the marina. With some fuel in the tank, we launched the boat. After a couple of pulls on the starter cord, my new boat mechanic friend coaxed the big 75 horsepower Yamaha two stroke into spluttering life.

The engine soon settled into a nice idle and, with a piece of coconut husk stuffed into the boat's drainage hole to stop it filling with water, we set off across the bay. The boat itself was a little rough around the edges - just what I needed as a work boat - but the engine sounded like it was in great shape.

I met the owner a couple of days later, and after a little haggling we struck a deal. We did some paperwork at the local notary office and I

Paradise Delayed

became a Panamanian boat owner. My first purchase at the marine hardware store was a drain plug, so I could replace the piece of rotting coconut husk that was currently filling the gap.

With the boat on the water, and a dock to use at the little hotel where I was staying, it was time to start learning a few boat handling skills. I was very lucky to have Eric with me during those early days, as I think the learning curve would have been liberally littered with more incidents and accidents. Eric was a cheery French Canadian guy who was possibly going to be leader of the team that would eventually build my house. He was going to help with the initial site preparation, and wanted to see the island.

On the first day we spent together, my first day with the boat, I offered to let him drive.

"No man. It's your boat. You have to learn how to use it, and how to avoid hitting things. Your boat is a pretty important part of your life down here."

So began my boat handling training course. It's all pretty straightforward if you think about it. The best piece of advice that Eric gave me was to take everything very slowly at first. When approaching a dock, it looks very impressive to turn up at top speed, like the local water taxi drivers, flick the engine into reverse at the last second, and coast to a stop right beside the dock. Gringos have a well documented history of trying such stunts without much success. You need to take your time to figure out what the water currents are doing and which way the wind may push the boat.

An extra complication thrown into the mix is that many boats, including my new purchase, are steered from the back. You have to sit beside the engine and move the engine itself to left or right by using the tiller handle. This is very counter-intuitive at first, and often results in dockside comedy.

However, before long I started to get used to the boat. The work crew I had gathered to take down to the island each day showed less and less fear of my docking skills as time went by.

Windy days always added further challenge. The spray blown in your face hampers visibility, as does the rain.

It was on a windy day that I made one of my more comedic mistakes. Heading north from the island towards town, I had inserted the engine cut-off key, which is supposed to operate like a dead man's handle on a train. Clipped to your lifejacket, if you fall overboard, the key is yanked out of the engine, and the motor stops running. In the boating world, there are a few horrific tales of hapless boaters falling overboard, only to have the unmanned boat turn in a circle and run the victim over.

So, I wisely had my cut-off clipped to my lifejacket. However, on this occasion, with the sun being out and only a light wind blowing over the calm water, I simply stuffed the lifejacket into the back of the boat beside the engine.

All went well for a while, until suddenly the engine cut out. I turned around to look at it, but couldn't initially see what was wrong. Then my vision caught sight of something orange on the water behind me. The boat was still moving forward, but friction with the water was slowing it gradually. The wind, coming from the north, was now blowing the lifejacket in my wake away to the south, along with the all-important cut-off key.

What to do? My mind raced through the options. The most obvious was to jump in and swim after the jacket. I started emptying my pockets of money and mobile phone. But with the boat still drifting in one direction and the jacket blowing in the other, the gap was widening. What if by the time I got there the gap was huge? Maybe I wouldn't make it back to the boat? But maybe the boat would start to drift back towards me in the water, carried by the wind. I wasn't really sure, but I knew that if I was going to swim it had to be now, before the lifejacket blew any further away.

I hesitated, still undecided. Could I just hold the cut-off switch out with my fingers, in the same way the key did? No, there was no way I could pull the starter cord with one hand. It was a big heavy engine to crank over. Something else then? A piece of wire perhaps, which could fill the gap?

I glanced around in the boat, and my eyes fell on a length of thin rope in one of the little storage compartments under the seats. There! That would do the trick. I fashioned a slip knot, placed it over the cut-off switch and pulled it tight. The engine started on the first pull, and I headed back to collect the lifejacket.

The first thing I did was put it on and fasten it up.

Log jam

"So *both* of the extra fuel cans are under the hatch?" Eric asked, looking at me incredulously. The question may have been punctuated by an expletive too.

"Er, yes," I answered sheepishly, looking at the dark, tumultuous sea heaving around us. We were in trouble.

An hour earlier, as we had loaded the boat, I hadn't thought to check how much fuel was left in the tank.

The relatively simple task for the day had been to go and collect some large logs Eric had had a local guy cut for us from his property. We were constructing wooden retaining walls so Eric could bring barge-loads of infill material to make a solid dock. He wanted to be able to bring a bobcat onto the island if he and his team were going to be building a house there in the near future.

Today was going to be one of my first major boat handling challenges. We had to collect the heavy logs and then transport them across the big open main bay of the archipelago to the island. When we had set out in the morning, the weather had been lovely, the sea calm. But as we headed into the bay with a boat laden to the gunnels with hefty logs, each measuring about 20 feet long, the skies looked ominously darker.

The boat is only 23 feet long from stem to stern. With the engine at the back, the logs had to be propped up on the bow, which made the boat a little top heavy.

I steered carefully, watching both the waves for any trouble ahead and the faces of my workers for any signs of fear. Both looked reasonably calm, and we made fairly decent progress.

But in worsening conditions, about midway across the bay, as the skies darkened and the seas built into a worryingly tumultuous mass of heaving water, things took a turn in an even more worrying direction. The engine coughed and spluttered, then died. All faces turned and looked at me expectantly, and I turned and looked down at the fuel can. A light tap with my foot confirmed my suspicions. "The tank's empty. How did that happen?"

"Well, hauling all of this weight means we've been burning much more fuel than usual," explained Eric. "We have got the two other cans, haven't we? Where are they?"

Oh, I knew exactly where they were. In the small locker, up at the front of the boat, which was buried under 24 heavy logs centred carefully in the boat. The lid of the locker opens upwards, and the logs were on top of the lid. I pointed forward.

"They're in there," I said quietly.

Maybe I said it too quietly. "What?" asked Eric incredulously.

"In there," I repeated, pointing once again at the obscured locker.

"So *both* of the extra fuel cans are under the hatch?"

"Er, yes."

"Okay," he sighed, and then began organising the three workers and myself calmly and efficiently. We shuffled logs carefully to left and right in the boat, or port and starboard if you want to be technical, being careful to maintain an even balance.

It was a tricky operation to pick the next log to move, trying to ensure that it wasn't entangled with others below it, or supporting others laid over part of it. We had to stack them carefully, making sure they would not move again, as we then had to clamber on top of the new piles, a couple of people on each side of the boat to maintain balance. It was like a real-life version of *Pick Up Sticks*.

As more logs were moved to the sides the boat became more unsteady, and the danger of the logs rolling increased too. There was a real potential for a crushed and broken leg if anything gave way. The thought of tipping the boat over, and ending up in the water under the logs didn't bear thinking about.

With infinite care in the rolling sea, we managed to clear the locker hatch, and freed the two five gallon petrol cans. They were sent down to the back of the boat, and the painstaking process of returning the wood to the centre of the boat began. We all heaved a sigh of relief when the wood was centred again, the fuel tank filled, and the engine restarted.

I had never been so glad to reach the end of a journey.

Language barriers

Once I had bought my boat, I needed to find a crew of workers. Between July, when I had finally become an island owner, and September, when I returned to try to make some sort of sense of my new purchase, I had sent Mark some money. He had promised he would get a couple of workers who helped him out on a regular basis to go and do some clearing at the island.

My first visit to the island confirmed the fact that, although some clearing had been done, there was much more work ahead.

My longer term plan was changing on a fairly regular basis, but broadly speaking, I wanted to completely clear the island of all the overgrown material. At the same time I needed to get some house plans drawn up. However, the first priority was to clear enough to be able to see most of the island, in order to be able to pick a site for the first building.

I wanted to initially build a small and basic, but comfortable and practical home. I wanted to do this quite quickly, and intended to build on a secondary location on the island. My idea was to then live in that, while I took my time to build what would become the main house on the property. The first house could then become either guest accommodation, or perhaps even a small rental place to provide some income.

I had settled in at Hotel Las Brisas, at the north end of the main street of Bocas Town, and had got to know the owner, Andy, fairly well. We had negotiated a weekly room rental deal, whereby I could keep my boat at his currently unused hotel dock too. I told him I was looking for workers, and asked his advice. He had plenty, much of it humorous and fairly cynical, based, he said, on many years experience.

He introduced me to Fernando, who did some occasional work at the hotel, and interpreted while I explained that I was looking for a few people who could handle machetes, to begin the clearing process. Fernando assured me he was the man for the job.

Andy had put the word out and the next day the hotel security guard asked me if I had some work for his nephew. Roman, the nephew, knew someone else also looking for work. Another guy, whom I met in the local restaurant, was also keen to join the team when he finished his current painting contract. Word seemed to spread like wildfire and there was a constant stream of applicants over the next day or so, asking if I was the gringo looking for workers. Before long I was collecting

Language barriers

telephone numbers and turning people away, as I had my initial team of four.

Much of my selection of workers had been based on word-of-mouth references, some much-appreciated interpretation from Andy, and many conversations in a mixture of Spanish and English. I had been studying some Spanish lessons I had on my computer, but still only had a rudimentary grasp of the language at best. Some of the potential workers spoke very little English, so I had employed Otis, as he could act as a bit of a go-between, his English being marginally better than my Spanish.

I had spoken at length with Eric about employment conditions, wages and work hours. I had come up with a basic premise that suited my needs, and involved very little, if any official paperwork.

Wages around town, for a worker who could swing a machete - something, it seemed, at which every Panamanian male over the age of 12 was very proficient at - were about $16 per day. On top of that, there was something called *'liquidación'*, which, as far as I could understand, was a 25% bonus paid at the end of a contract. This made daily wages the equivalent of $20. After three months of contracted work, there were extra bonuses, holiday pay, time off, and other complications, all of which were governed by local employment laws. Most long-term employers had to pay an agent to look after contracts and wage payments, incurring further costs.

I came up with a much simpler plan. As I didn't expect to need anyone for three months, I decided to simply work a cash-in-hand system. I would employ people on a casual day-to-day basis, paying the full $20 at the end of each day's work, which would include the equivalent of the *'liquidación'* 25% bonus. This seemed to cause some confusion at times among my new team, but when Otis grasped the concept and explained it to the others, all were happy with the arrangement.

It turned out that there were several benefits to my system. The standard working day was eight hours, 8am to 4pm. This included travel time to and from work, which I was obviously providing in my recently purchased boat, a one hour lunch break, and lunch that the employees hoped that the *jefe* (boss-man) would provide. Eric told me that many workers would not bring any lunch with them, and if unfed, would fade mid-afternoon.

"Feed 'em well if you want a good day's work," was his advice.

Punctuality was one of the first problems that I had to tackle. Turning up ready for work at 8am didn't always seem to be a priority. On the first few days, we were departing at 8.15 or 8.20am from the hotel. After the

Paradise Delayed

first week, when the departure time started to get pushed further back, I'd had enough. In my muddled Spanish, with some help from Otis, I explained that the boat would be leaving the hotel dock at exactly 8am. Anyone not there wouldn't be working that day, and of course, wouldn't be paid that day.

"Is that fair?" I had asked. All agreed that it was, and punctuality improved significantly.

Occasionally the day would begin with pouring rain, and we would wait at the hotel to see if things were going to clear up, playing cards and drinking coffee. If the rain was still pounding down by 9 or 10am, I'd suggest we call it a day, and I would pay a half day's wages.

"Is that fair?" I had asked again. Indeed it was, all agreed.

My first firing wasn't long in coming. The guy I had met in the restaurant had finished his painting contract and had come to work for a couple of days, increasing my team to five. There was plenty of work to go around. However, he seemed to have more issues than most of the others with punctuality and missed the boat several mornings. Time to implement a new rule, I thought - three strikes and you are out. My one-day's-work-for-one-day's-pay policy offered flexibility for both sides of the employment agreement. I was happy to let someone have a day off if they let me know in advance - I could either replace them for the day, or reduce the lunch supplies I needed to buy that morning. However, if someone just didn't show, I'd give them a couple of chances. On the third no-show they were out of a job. I asked my usual question.

"Is that fair?"

"That fair," agreed Otis, laughing. "Me think Armando him like de weed too much. Him not be back again anyhow." Sure enough, my first worker had fired himself without input from me, and the others became very punctual indeed.

I continued to work on my Spanish, trying to squeeze in an audio lesson before work and, if not too tired, another after work. But it was with my work crew that I really began to learn to communicate. They taught me the words for all the tools we used, as well as a few colourful local phrases. I asked them all to feel free to correct me when I said something wrong. They would ask me how to say some things in English, and we began to build quite a rapport.

We worked hard for a couple of months and slowly the island began to reveal its secrets. I worked side-by-side with my team and I think I gained a degree of respect from them - apparently not too many of the

Language barriers

gringos put in a full day alongside their local workers, let alone a couple of months.

When rain prevented work at the island I worked on a house design. I employed a local architect to draw out plans and get all the necessary permissions.

After three months the initial clearing work was almost done. On one memorable occasion, as I was marking out a potential house site, I overheard Fernando chatting to one of the other guys. He pointed around the island at the work we had been doing.

"Sera un paraiso," he said - it will be a paradise.

I too looked around and felt pride at what we had achieved. It was now possible to see right across the island, and to walk across it too. The potential was obvious, and I was very happy.

The next day was our last together, as I was heading to Colorado to meet up with Moe and the kids. They were coming down to join me for three months in Bocas, avoiding the worst of Whitehorse's deep, dark winter. We only worked for half a day. At lunch time I broke out a case of icy chilled beer from the cold lunch box and we celebrated our achievements.

I had thoroughly enjoyed working with my local team and learning something of their lives. They were always quick to laugh, worked hard, and had a pride in what they did. My Spanish had improved greatly, and I felt that I had overcome many of the early barriers in fine style.

Chainsaw challenges

On the island, clearing efforts were progressing well. It was now becoming possible to mark out potential pathways and consider house locations. However, the clearing work had also revealed many dead trees which would need to be felled. My plan was to buy a chainsaw. I had used one on several occasions up in Whitehorse, under Moe's expert guidance, and felt ready to tackle my own timber issues.

Andy, the owner/manager at Las Brisas Hotel, suggested that I should look online at the bigger Panamanian hardware stores, as he was flying to Panama City in a day or two, and could bring a chainsaw back for me.

Everyone I spoke to suggested I needed either a Stihl or a Husqvarna, but quality comes at a price and neither of these two brands are particularly cheap options. I didn't have too many trees, and once they were removed, other than for very occasional use, I didn't expect to have much further need for a chainsaw. It wouldn't be anything like Whitehorse, where Moe had to cut about six cords of wood to get through each winter.

So against advice I went for a cheaper option, made by Hyundai. When Andy returned with the shiny new tool, it certainly looked the part, and once I got it running at the island, the trees started to fall without too much trouble. I tackled the smaller dead lumber first, and all went well for a while. With growing confidence, some of the larger trees fell too, and I strode confidently towards one of the biggest trees in the centre of the island.

The saw performed well on the first cut, but as I began the second, the engine, running at high revs, just cut out. It took a bit of pulling and cajoling to remove the saw from the tree, and I tried to restart it. Nothing. When I removed the spark plug, grounding it on the head of the engine, there was no sign of a spark. Something seemed to have given up in the electrical system.

Back in town I spoke to Andy, Eric, and a couple of other people. Andy had his mechanic take a look, but it was obvious that if we started to take too much apart, I would void the warranty. Andy rang the hardware store where he had bought the saw, and was told that to exchange it under warranty, it needed to come back to the store. "How do I get this thing back to Panama City?" I asked him, pointing to the oily tool covered in sawdust that sat on the hotel reception desk.

"We'll put it on the plane tomorrow, and I'll have a taxi driver that does some work for me collect it and drop it off at the store."

I drained as much of the remaining petrol as I could out the small fuel tank. I left it open to dry out, standing the chainsaw on some plastic bags in the bathroom. My bedroom was already full of tools which were transported on a daily basis to the island, along with a large insulated container for drinks and food. It was a good job that I was out at the island most days, otherwise the cleaning lady would have some challenges getting around the bed.

The chainsaw still had a bit of a whiff of fuel about it, so I opened the windows in the bathroom and closed the door, hoping that the smell wouldn't reach the rooms next door. I was already pushing my luck at the hotel, what with the boat at the dock, the workers traipsing through the lobby each day, and the muddy tools in the bedroom.

In the morning I wrapped the useless item in its original packaging, and Andy took me in his little beach buggy to the airport, just a couple of blocks away. I was concerned that the saw it would not be allowed in the hold, because there had been fuel in it. I once had a camping stove burner, which used methylated spirits, confiscated before a flight. However, there were no such worries with the Panamanian airline. The clerk simply weighed the parcel, took some details, and charged the very reasonable sum of $15.

It took several days, but a brand new replacement saw finally arrived. I resolved to use it in short bursts only, hoping to nurse it along through the remainder of the tree felling work at the island.

Things didn't start too well, as there were problems with the second saw from the outset. The engine started fine and ran well, but the system that feeds lubricating oil to the chain didn't seem to function at all. I checked what I could and fiddled with any wires and tubes I could access, but couldn't get the oil to flow. I eventually resolved the problem by carrying a small container of lubricating oil with me from tree to tree, dipping the chain in it frequently to stop it from drying out. It wasn't a perfect solution, but it meant I could make some progress, despite the oil thrown off the chain all over my clothes.

After twenty minutes of productive work and satisfying crashes of trees falling, I experienced a horrible moment of déjà vu. While cutting through a larger trunk, the saw simply stopped, just as the last one had. On further examination, it exhibited the same symptoms as the previous one. With the job only half done at most, my second saw was dead.

"Tell 'em I don't want it replaced," I told Andy, as he spoke again with the store in Panama City. "It's a piece of junk."

Paradise Delayed

Covering the mouthpiece of the phone, he explained that the saw would have to go back to the store in Panama City. From there it would be sent to the company's repair and assessment facility before they would decide whether to repair, replace or refund.

"Refund!" I demanded. "I don't want another one!"

"It's going to take a week or two," Andy explained, translating the answer from the store.

I went through the whole rigmarole of emptying the fuel again, and re-packaged the saw, taking it to the airport once again the next morning.

At breakfast, after dropping off the saw, I chatted with Ryan, the young guy who ran the little café in the hotel foyer, telling him of my chainsaw challenges.

"Should have bought a Stihl. Or maybe a Husqvarna," he suggested brightly, laughing.

"Yeah, thanks Ryan. Just pour the coffee mate."

Engine issues

I met up with Moe, Finn and Maible at Denver airport, catching them completely by surprise. They thought I'd be meeting them several days later at San Jose airport in Costa Rica, but they had planned a few days skiing and snowboarding with friends of ours at Copper Mountain and I hadn't wanted to miss out.

By the time they arrived at Denver late in the evening they were worn out after many hours of travel. They still had to collect a hire car and drive another couple of hours through a raging snowstorm, to the mountain condo that would be home for the weekend.

Moe just looked at me blankly when she first saw me, unable to quite process how or why I was there. When the shock wore off, she hugged me happily. We hadn't seen each other for several months, so the early reunion was very welcome. On top of that, when she realised that I already had a car, and she didn't have to drive, she was so relieved.

The short winter break was fantastic fun, but I was happy to return to the sunny warmth of Panama. We had rented a large house in town for the first month, as we had several visitors booked to come and see us from various parts of the globe. There were going to be nine of us there over Christmas.

At the house we had rented we met the first of our guests. I had met Peter several years ago, as I passed through Germany on my goal achieving adventure, and we had stayed in touch. Craig and Gemma were also in town and soon arrived at the house too. Craig has been a friend since my early days in Australia, and we have ensured our paths have crossed as often as possible.

My brother Martin, along with partner Rachel, was next to arrive, filling the house to the brim. Peter had to spend a couple of nights in a hammock, as all the beds were full.

On the first sunny Sunday morning we took a trip south in my boat, looking for the fabled jungle restaurant Rana Azul, which translates to English as "Blue Frog". Craig and Gemma wanted to check out the amazing Bocas surf, so declined to join us. The rest of us headed for Hotel Las Brisas, where my boat was still moored.

When she saw the boat, Rachel flatly refused to get in. 'It's tiny," she said. "It doesn't look at all stable." No amount of persuasion would change her mind, and she eventually elected to look around town. Maybe read her book for a while back at the house, swinging in a hammock.

Paradise Delayed

Martin wasn't about to miss out on the trip, and joined us in the boat, waving goodbye to Rachel as we departed.

About halfway into the journey the boat began to cough and splutter a little, misfiring occasionally. I knew it wasn't a shortage of fuel on this occasion, as I had just filled the tank before departing from town. I kicked the tank lightly, confirming it was still more than half full.

Fortunately, one of the most important boating lessons Eric taught me was to always carry tools in the boat, as you never know when you're going to need them. The basics include a selection of spanners, including an adjustable one, and a couple of different types of screwdriver. The most vital things to have are a spark plug spanner and a new set of spark plugs.

The further we went, the worse the engine seemed to get. It sounded like one of the spark plugs was now misfiring badly, so we pulled up, switched off the engine, and I rooted around in the locker for the tool kit.

"Maybe its better that Rachel didn't come with us," said Maible. All agreed that she was probably right.

The spark plug spanner was a little rusty from the damp salty atmosphere in the locker, but was still serviceable. The new spark plugs were fine, as I had thought to wrap then in plastic. As I took the plugs out of the engine one by one I discovered that the plug from the bottom of the three cylinders was very wet with water, not fuel. I replaced the plug with a new one and we were off again.

Five minutes later the engine started misfiring again. We went through the whole rigmarole once more, again finding the bottom plug to be very wet. I was starting to think that I must have a problem with the head gasket.

"We should head home," I suggested, "before we do any further damage to the engine."

The trip home was long and tedious, frequently interrupted by stops to clean and dry the offending spark plug. We eventually made it and I parked the boat up, planning to buy a new head gasket and find a mechanic the next day.

However, with Christmas fast approaching a mechanic was difficult to pin down. Most seemed keener on celebrating the festive season than dealing with oily engines. With my brother and other friends visiting, I decided to let the engine wait until after the New Year and joined the Christmas festivities.

By the time a mechanic came to look at the engine, it had sat unused for a couple of weeks.

"Before we pull the head off I want to look at the exhaust. The problem could be in there. It is a common issue with this engine model."

He started stripping the engine down while it was still docked at the hotel, thankfully with the permission of Andy, the friendly gringo hotel owner, as it wasn't too long before parts were scattered all over the dock. The problem was in the exhaust system. The fire plate, which separates the hot exhaust gases from the water which cools the engine, had a small hole. This was allowing water to leak back into the bottom cylinder via the exhaust.

This would have been a simple problem to resolve, if the engine hadn't been stood with salty water in it for a couple of weeks. By now the cylinders had seized in the barrels, and the engine would need a full stripdown to bring it back to working condition.

"We'll have to take the cylinder head off to see how bad it is - no problem though, as you already have a new head gasket."

He undid the bolts, and pulled the cylinder head off. He looked at the engine silently for a second or two, the breathed two words you really don't want to hear from your mechanic.

"Oh wow!"

"I'm guessing that's not wow-good, is it?" I asked.

"No. We're going to have to take the engine block to my boss's workshop to do any more with it."

Even my untrained mechanical eyes could see that he was right. It was a brown rusty mess inside the engine. The engine block was duly removed and transported in my wheelbarrow to the workshop just along the street. There it was further stripped, and the boss mechanic did some rough calculations.

"New crank, big end bearings, piston and rings, small end bearings, full gasket set, several hours of labour. My guess is about three thousand dollars," he quoted glibly. I was pretty sure I could just buy another second-hand engine for that price.

"Put it all back in the wheelbarrow," I said. "I guess it's just scrap now."

"Ahh, wait a minute," said the big boss mechanic. "Maybe we could get away without a new crank. That would bring it down to two thousand."

"In the wheelbarrow," I repeated.

"We could try to re-use the pistons, but I couldn't guarantee the work. Maybe fifteen hundred?" he suggested hopefully. I didn't trust this guy at all and felt like he was trying for the biggest price he could. It appeared he was now simply lowering the price to find out how much I was willing to pay. I wanted a second opinion.

I gathered the rest of the pieces of my sad looking engine, which now more resembled a small rusty junkyard in a wheelbarrow than an engine. I headed out onto the street along with Juancho, one of my main workers.

"Now what, Juancho? Who can we try next?"

"We go see Papa D," proclaimed Juancho. "He real good mechanic. Old guy. Real cheap too."

"Okay, Papa D sounds like the man to see."

Papa D lived down one of the small side streets off the main street. His front yard was a jumble of smaller engines in various states of disassembly. Juancho introduced me to the wizened old man who appeared from the debris of his front garden workshop. Papa D gazed at the rusty metal in my wheel barrow.

"Big engine, 75 horse," he proclaimed. At least he knew what the parts were from without being told, which was a promising start. "I not work on de big engines no more. Too heavy for me." Not so promising.

But his gnarled mechanic's hands strayed into the wheelbarrow as I explained what had happened to the engine. "Dis crank okay," he declared. "And de piston barrels dem clean up okay. Dis not need many parts to fix." He continued to pull parts out of the wheelbarrow and scrutinise them. "Dis good. Dis we need new one. Dis okay, maybe no, but we need clean to be sure." He was obviously becoming enthused about the project, and his use of the word "we" was very encouraging.

I knew enough to stay quiet and let him continue to muse over the parts. "Yes, we can fix him." My engine now had a gender and the mechanic was keen. "I tink maybe one hundred fifty parts, and I charge one fifty labour."

Three hundred dollars! Coming on the heels of a three thousand dollar estimate, I was over the moon. Papa D was employed on the spot. "I order de parts tomorrow, dem come from Panama on de plane in de afternoon, I start work de next day."

Within a week the engine was rebuilt, reinstated back on the boat by the younger mechanic who had taken it off in the first place, and with strict

Engine issues

instructions from Papa D to "run him in gentle-like", we were back on the water.

The parts had even come in at slightly less than the hundred and fifty dollars originally quoted, so my whole bill was under three hundred. Marvellous!

The engine ran well and I did "run him in gentle-like".

Over the following months the boat worked hard, transporting all sorts of odd loads during the initial house construction and completion, and for the development of the cleared island - bags of cement, wood, plants and much more. It gave me over a year of almost trouble free use, before I eventually traded it for something less workhorse-like when the house build was completed.

"There's water coming in at the front!"

The bulk of the island clearing was now finished, and the construction of my storage shed was nearing its conclusion, with only the doors still to be mounted. Just days before Christmas the engine on the boat burned a hole through an integral part of the exhaust system, and salt water had filled the bottom cylinder, resulting in time-consuming repair work.

So with little else to do at the island, and no boat to get there anyway, we enjoyed a Caribbean Christmas with extended family and friends who had travelled to visit us. It's funny - I had spent two summers up in Whitehorse, and only one friend had made it up there to visit. Now that I was the proud owner of a Caribbean island we had more than half a dozen visitors within the first three months.

Some of our guests headed home after the holidays, but those remaining were still keen to see the property, and, and I needed to figure out a way to get us all there. Fortune favoured us when one day I spotted Napoleon, who had done much of the initial clearing work at the island, working with a petrol-powered weed-whacker on the property next door to our rental house.

I chatted with him for a while, and he mentioned that he knew of another small island property for sale somewhere near mine. Was I interested in taking a look, he wondered? I explained that my boat was out of action, and he was quick to explain that his family owned a big kayuko, one of the local-style wooden boats hollowed out of a tree trunk. Kayukos vary in size, anywhere from a small single person kayak, to monster boats with outboards capable of carrying a dozen people. Would Napo's boat take six of us, I asked? Indeed it would, he assured me. We arranged to meet the next morning to view his cousin's property, as well as visit my island to show our friends around.

Napo's boat was indeed big enough for the six of us, plus himself at the back to drive. It had obviously seen better days, but looked to be in fairly reasonable shape. It was powered by a little 15 horsepower engine, and with us all aboard, it pottered along at a good pace.

The property Napo showed us was pretty small, perhaps about a tenth of the size of my island, and his estimated price was more than I had paid for my property. It wasn't something in which I was going to be interested. Onward to our island.

We wandered around the island, and our friends made the appropriate oohs and ahhs as we explained plans, showing them where the house was

"There's water coming in at the front"

going to be built. The land still needed much work to finish the cleaning and tidying process. It would still be a couple of years before the pineapples, bananas and other fruit trees that I had planted would really begin to develop fully, so you still had to use some imagination and vision to see how it might all look one day.

Our visit over, we all climbed back into Napo's boat for the journey back to town. As is often the case, the wind had come up in the afternoon. The sea was a little choppy for the return journey, but was by no means rough. The boat handled the swell without any problems, and all seemed to be going well, when a message came back down the line from the bow. "The boat is splitting open. There's water coming in at the front!"

Kayukos are long and narrow, and in this case was only wide enough to sit single file along the length. I had sat in front of Napo so I could talk to him as we puttered along. In front of me Moe sat with Maible, and ahead of her were our friends Heather and Sean. Up at the bow Finn was the initiator of the message, and I tried to see past all of the people to find out what was going on. At least there didn't seem to be any panic, and Finn looked quite calm.

As I craned my neck to get a better look Finn turned around to look forward again, then turned back once more, this time looking a lot less calm than he had at first. His eyes were huge and round, and he leaned to his side so I could see the front of the boat past him.

There was no exaggeration, the boat was indeed splitting open. A sizeable gap had opened in the bow, where the wood had split open along the grain, which ran along the length of the bow. As each successive wave hit the front of the boat the split was being forced wider, and more water was rushing in.

I turned back to Napo, and without time to mentally construct what I wanted to say in Spanish, I tried to explain what was happening up front. By the time I started getting my garbled message across explanation had become redundant, as the water was rising around us extremely quickly.

Napo closed the throttle and stood up to take a look at the damage. Panic was starting to spread up at the front of the boat, which was by now close to being completely under water. Napo acted swiftly and calmly, turning the boat to the left. This meant the waves were now catching us on the right side, and were no longer forcing the split open, but in fact holding it closed.

The action in the boat was frantic. I had visions of it sinking quickly, taking Napo's family's engine with it to the bottom. We were out in deep water, about half way between the island and town. I quickly scanned the

Paradise Delayed

horizon, but couldn't see any other boats. If we all ended up swimming it could be quite a while until another boat passed by. The water wasn't too cold, but a long time in it could still potentially result in hypothermia.

Behind me Napo started calmly bailing water out, while Moe tried to calm the people up ahead. Heather had sat up on the edge of the boat, out of the rising water, and Moe was trying to tell her to get back in the bottom of the boat to keep our centre of gravity low.

We had a gallon of drinking water with us in an insulated container. I quickly spun the lid off, ditching the chilled fresh water overboard, and started bailing seawater out as quickly as I could.

Maible was up on her feet directly in front of me, asking her mum if we should jump overboard, already keen to abandon the floundering boat.

"No, not yet. It's all going to be okay," Moe reassured her.

I was having some problems bailing, as Maible's feet and legs were in my way. I asked her to climb over her mother and head forward slightly, but got no response. I looked up at her and saw that her face was frozen in shock and fear.

Moe had spotted the problem too, and was talking to Maible calmly, trying to get her to move forward. I couldn't move back, as Napo was bailing behind me.

I said to Moe, "You need to get her to move now."

Maible was literally frozen in fear. I had always thought this was a figure of speech, but she just couldn't seem to respond.

Moe had to grab one of her feet and move it herself, then help her move the other leg. Despite the situation I was amazed and fascinated. As soon as I had enough room I began bailing, while up ahead others used a cup and an empty oil container.

As we bailed a hasty discussion took place. We agreed that someone needed to know about our predicament. Mark, the ever helpful real estate agent and friend, seemed to be the most obvious choice. I passed my bailer to Moe and retrieved my phone from its plastic bag and called him, catching him at his office. With all of the noise in the boat, and the engine running just behind me, it was difficult to hear his responses. I managed to explain our situation, giving him our approximate location.

"Can you hear me okay Mark?" I shouted into the phone. "If I don't call you exactly one hour from now, our boat has sunk, and we are all treading water out here in the middle of the bay. Got that?

"There's water coming in at the front"

Mark confirmed that he understood, and would be ready to come out to look for us, as well as alert others if he didn't hear from us at the appointed time. I returned to bailing, explaining to the others what I had told Mark. There was another hasty, panicky conference, Heather being adamant that we needed someone to be coming out right now. I wasn't sure. We seemed to be at least maintaining the water level in the boat now, if not yet lowering it. Napo seemed very calm, bailing casually, as if this was an everyday occurrence for him. Maybe it was?

Heather was insistent though, and with Maible still looking very traumatised, it did seem like a reasonable precaution to take.

I phoned Mark again. "Yep, we might be going down here," I explained. "Even if we don't, it might be a good idea to get a few people out of the boat." Over the noise, it sounded like Mark said he was on his way. I hoped the message had got through.

We all continued bailing, and for a while the water level didn't change. For a couple of long minutes we seemed to teeter on the brink of tipping the boat over, or having it simply sink from beneath us. However, slowly at first, we started to see progress as the water level began to drop, and it became apparent that we were winning. The relief all around was quite evident.

When the water was only a few inches deep, Napo put the engine into gear, and we started forward again. Initially he tried turning directly towards town, but the first wave opened the split again, sending a sickening roll of water down the inside of the boat. More frantic bailing emptied the boat again as Napo angled us across the waves once more.

It seemed that if we continued at a slight angle across the waves we could limit the amount of water entering the boat, and our bailing efforts could easily remove the water at the same rate it was coming in. We shuffled people back down the boat as far as we could in order to raise the bow. It would still be quite some time before Mark would get to us, as he would have to either go home and get his boat out, or find a water taxi in town that could bring him out. Hopefully we could stay afloat until then, so long as the damage to the front of the boat didn't get any worse.

Napo handled the boat skilfully, and we made progress carefully northwards. The further we travelled, the more we came into the lee of the main island, and before too long Napo could open the throttle a little wider without the bow crashing into the tops of the waves. Eventually we made it to calmer waters. Now fully sheltered by the main island, we could turn directly towards town again.

We were almost there when my phone rang.

Paradise Delayed

"I'm on my way now," Mark told me.

I explained where we now were, approaching town from the south west end near the marina. We managed to figure out that we were pretty close to each other, and co-ordinated a rendezvous on the water. By the time Mark found us it was pretty obvious that we were now going to get back safely, and we all thanked him profusely for coming to our potential rescue.

Napo docked the boat at the south end of town and I paid him for the day's excursion, adding a decent tip for the safe return of his charges.

"Call me if there is anything I can do to help with the boat repairs," I told him. He didn't seem particularly disconcerted by the whole experience, grinning happily.

Back at the house the kids elected to stay at home and get showered off. Moe and I went out to the local store and bought a large pack of chilled beer to take round to Mark's office to celebrate being safely back on dry land.

House roof underwater

Towards the end of my first three months of island clearing Juancho had proved to be an invaluable addition to my team. He had been highly recommended as a very capable worker by young ex-pat surfer Ryan, who ran the café at Hotel Las Brisas and who also owned property in the archipelago.

I originally hired Juancho because he owned several chainsaws, and our clearing work had revealed many dead trees and stumps that would need to be removed. My efforts with the unreliable Hyundai chainsaws had resulted in two broken machines, several trips back and forth to the airport, and the job only half done.

Juancho turned up at the island, and with his trusty saw, a Stihl of course, made very short work of the remaining dead lumber. Within a couple of days everything was on the ground, chopped up into manageable pieces which my team of workers either burned or gathered into a big pile of future firewood.

Juancho was keen to work, and with no further commitments, was keen to show off his chainsaw skills. He had cut several amazingly smooth and straight planks out of one of the larger trees he had felled.

Pointing at the dilapidated main dock he suggested, "I fix this. New wood, new roof at the end. My brother have big farm with many trees... phew, big trees. We cut planks from trees, bring here, new dock. Finish very nice."

We discussed prices, materials and time scales, coming to an arrangement that seemed to make both of us very happy, and Juancho was employed for a further week. After that he moved on to fixing the secondary dock, having done a marvellous job on the main dock, and his employment was extended again.

By this time the lumber I had ordered for the initial dwelling I wanted to build had arrived in Bocas, and I needed somewhere to store it on the island.

"You need to build big bodega. I build for you. Strong and secure." Juancho suggested. He was proving to be a skilled jack-of-all-trades. The next day he introduced me to a couple of other gringos for whom he had done work. They were very happy to give him a glowing recommendation. Again we haggled and negotiated, and again we both seemed very happy with the agreement to which we came.

Paradise Delayed

Juancho had by now become the leader of my team of workers. He gathered a few more guys to help with the construction of the storage shed, or bodega, as everyone tended to call it. Bags of concrete were brought in, along with huge amounts of sand and gravel. I gave Juancho the go-ahead to start construction, just as I headed off for a week to meet up with Moe and the kids. They were stopping over in snowy Colorado for a few days as they headed south to join me, avoiding the worst of the chilly Canadian winter months, and planned on doing some snowboarding and skiing with friends there. I didn't want to miss out.

The bodega was almost complete by the time we all returned to Bocas, but I noticed immediately that it was built as a mirror image of the plans I had left with Juancho. I had mapped out a large concrete slab on which the shed would sit on the left side, the right side being open space under the roof. The building before me sat on the right side of the slab with the open space to the left. I looked at the finished result in slight amazement - I was pretty sure my explanations and drawings had been quite clear, but here was the evidence that they had obviously not been as clear as I had thought.

Before saying anything I realised that it really didn't make any difference at all. Raising the issue would achieve nothing but embarrass Juancho in front of his proud team, and sour our growing working relationship. It certainly was a fine-looking shed. I did vaguely remember Eric's advice about always being on site when local workers were constructing anything, and decided to follow this advice a little more closely, should there be a next time.

There was a bit of a debacle with the doors, which had been fabricated by a guy in Almirante that Juancho had guaranteed did quality work. The doors that showed up were thin and flimsy, nothing like what I had ordered. Apparently there had been some mix up in delivery, and I was assured that I had received someone else's doors by mistake. I was very sceptical, as they fitted my shed exactly. I suspected it was a case of trying to palm off poorer quality doors on an unsuspecting gringo. Juancho promised to remedy the situation, and within a week I had doors that looked much more like those I had specified.

Of course Juancho had quizzed me about future plans, asking about the possibility of building the house. I was still verbally half-committed to Eric and his team, but they had quoted North American building prices to me. While I was sure I was going to get great quality construction - I had seen much of their work - it wasn't going to come cheap.

I wanted to build a smallish house to act as a first residence on the island. I had selected the site which I thought would be the best position for the

House roof underwater

main island home, but didn't intend to build there yet. I planned to first build what would eventually become visitors' accommodation, in a different location, away from what would ultimately be the site for the main house. Therefore I really didn't want to spend too much on this first dwelling.

Juancho and I spent some time with sheets of paper, along with the house plans I had now received from the architect in town, as we worked on a proposal for him to lead a team to build the house. The price on which we eventually agreed was about a third of what I would be paying the Canadian guys, and again I consulted with some of Juancho's previous customers. Satisfied that he would do a good job, we shook hands, and my house builder was hired. We had agreed that he was going to pick his own team and arrange transport and food for them. They would use the bodega as sleeping accommodation while the construction was underway.

I spoke with Eric, broaching the subject of having someone else build my house.

"Whew, that's a relief man," was his happy response. "We have so many big jobs on at the moment. I've been worrying about how we were going to manage to do your place too. The only thing is you'll need to get your lumber out of the yard if we're not doing the job for you."

"Yep, no problem," I agreed confidently, without a clue how to move so much timber down to the island. It would take at least ten trips in my boat, and to be honest, I'd had enough of that sort of adventure after the log jam fiasco.

"No problem. We use Toño, him have big-big boat," Juancho suggested. As well as being an accomplished jack-of-all-trades, Juancho had lived in Bocas all his life and seemed to know just about everyone. He had certainly become my number one go-to-guy with any problem I had.

Toño did indeed have a big boat - it was huge. It was one of the biggest kayukos in the islands, Toño told me proudly, and I believed him. Constructed from one enormous hollowed out tree trunk with extra planking to build up the sides, pushed along by a 40 horsepower motor, it was capable of moving extremely heavy loads.

On the big day Juancho brought his team of guys to supplement the workers Toño had with him. Along with the guys from the Canadians' yard who had a truck, we ferried wood to the big boat and loaded it to the gunnels. Toño figured that if we got enough in the first time, we could shift the rest of it in one more journey.

Paradise Delayed

For the first trip to the island I was going to have to navigate, as Toño hadn't been before, and Juancho had his own boat to transport his own team of guys. In the big, heavily laden kayuko Toño strongly suggested we keep as low as possible to keep the centre of gravity down. As he pulled slowly away from the dock I found a place in the bottom of the boat among the other workers.

As we picked up speed in the direction of the island the big boat rolled sickeningly on the light swell, but the guys around me looked relaxed and at ease. I couldn't help but think that I was now in the bottom of what was basically a big log, several tons of wood balanced precariously above me, on a sea that although calm, wasn't flat by any means. If this thing rolls over, I thought, we don't have a chance under all that weight of wood. Although I tried to look relaxed among the others, I was mentally prepared to scramble forward as quickly as possible if things took a turn for the worse.

My fears were groundless, and the journey passed without incident, the wood quickly being unloaded and packed neatly into the shed. I breathed a sigh of relief when Toño said he didn't need me to navigate for the second trip.

I contracted him to bring sand, gravel and cement in the quantities Juancho specified. He delivered those the following day, and we were ready to commence construction.

Water was no longer a problem, as Juancho had set up collection pipes from the roof of the bodega, and we had several full barrels. I had bought a 600 gallon water tank in town, and Juancho brought it down to the island in his brother's big kayuko. When connected to the roof pipes, it provided drinking water, with plenty to spare for the concrete foundations of the house.

I was living in town with Moe and the kids, and we had had several visitors during that time. However, mindful of Eric's advice, and learning from previous experiences, I spent as much time as I could at the island overseeing the proceedings. I didn't really know what I was looking for, but felt my presence did help in keeping things smoothly on track. Juancho often had questions on how I wanted things done, and we did manage to catch a few things that may have been done differently to what I had envisioned, had I not been there.

The foundation work took quite some time. Once done had to be left for a week to dry and harden before further work continued. However, once the wood came out of the shed the frame of the house took shape very quickly.

House roof underwater

"We need tin for roof by de end of de week," Juancho informed me, and we arranged to meet at the supplier in Almirante to place an order.

We went to collect it a couple of days later. I took a water taxi from town to meet Juancho, once more in his brother's kayuko, in order to transport the roof material to the island.

We needed over forty sheets of the corrugated tin material, each sheet being sixteen feet long by four feet wide. They weren't too heavy individually, but as the guys in the warehouse stacked our order up it was obvious that the whole pile was quite a significant weight. Juancho was breezily confident that the boat could handle it. Our order was transported via forklift to the little dock where we could load it into the boat.

I had picked coloured material, choosing the commonly used red. I didn't want to scratch any of the paint off, so had Juancho make sure his guys understood that we had to load it carefully. The first piece, being wider than the boat's width, had to be carefully curled into the bottom of the hull, the following pieces being added on top one-by-one. As the weight of the little boat increased it settled deeper into the water, and I was quietly pleased that I would be going back to town in a water taxi - I'd had my fill of over-laden boat trips by now.

We had to work slowly as the edges and corners of the tin sheets were wickedly sharp. Sliding a hand along an edge would result in serious injury. After moving the first couple of sheets I went back into the store to buy gloves for all of us, my hands already marked by several small nicks.

As we loaded one of the sheets, about a third of the way through the process, another boat went past the dock, causing our boat to rock on the waves of the wake it left behind. I was at the back of the growing pile of tin, one of Juancho's workers was at the front, and Juancho was on the dock passing the tin down to us. The two of us in the boat stopped moving, steadied the boat easily until the rolling stopped, then prepared to receive the next sheet. Unfortunately, the right side of the boat had slipped under the dock as the waves had rocked us, and was now caught firmly under there, wedging the boat into place. We looked at the problem, wondering if we needed to free the boat now, or try when it was full.

"Safer to free now," decided Juancho, and I had no desire to question his lifetime of boat handling experience.

Paradise Delayed

The pair of us in the boat moved our combined weight over to the right side of the boat, pushing against the dock. The boat was stuck fast. Juancho tried joining us to push too, but the results were the same.

"Maybe if we find something to lever against the boat at the front there," I suggested.

Juancho found a sturdy piece of wood. With two of us in the boat pushing, and Juancho levering from above the side of the boat scraped slowly out from under the concrete dock. As it suddenly popped up, free from constraint, both of us in the boat were thrown across to the left side, and the tin shifted sickeningly between us. We both tried scrambling back towards the dock, but gravity and momentum were against us, and the tin was picking up speed.

I experienced one of those incredible moments of clarity, when time seems to slow down, giving your brain a chance process all sorts of possible outcomes in the blink of an eye. I have only had it happen once before in such a crystal clear fashion, when a dog ran out in front of the motorbike I was riding. As it happened I seemed to have all the time in the world to decide how to react to avoid the potential accident. I was aware of cars in front of me, cars behind, cars approaching from the other direction and the dog's path and speed. The decision to swerve to the right seemed obvious, and worked perfectly. Afterwards, half a mile down the road I had pulled the bike up, shaking from the after effects of the huge dump of adrenaline into my system, absolutely stunned at how quickly my brain had processed all the information when under pressure.

The moment in the boat, as everything seemed suspended in time in delicate balance, was very similar to the moment on the motorbike. Many possibilities were clear, the difference this time being that I knew there was nothing I could do to stop the tin going over the side. The fact that was most clear was that if one of the pieces caught my leg as it went, the injury would be horrific. The razor sharp edge would cut flesh as easily as a sharp knife cuts a watermelon. My decision, seemingly made with all the time in the world, was to grab the right edge of the boat and curl my legs up quickly. I did not reach out to grab the tin, as automatic reaction might dictate. That would certainly have resulted in a lost finger or two.

As if in slow motion, the boat tipped further, the tin slipping almost majestically over the side, my legs now well clear. All of the tin went, and amazingly, as the last sheet slipped over the edge, the boat popped back upright without even gathering up any water. The pair of us in the boat looked at each other wide eyed. We were both okay, untouched by the sharp tin, and obviously very relieved.

House roof underwater

We all leaned over the left side of the boat and gazed into the murky water. The seabed dropped off pretty steeply from the dock, the water dark and uninviting. There was no sign of the tin, and I didn't relish the thought of going in there to try to retrieve it.

"Good grief! What do we do now?" I wondered out loud in despair.

"This no big problem," Juancho said confidently. "I borrow mask, we go down and get roof out of water, not take long."

My thoughts didn't match his confidence and I expressed my doubts, but Juancho was already on his phone to a friend who lived nearby, and a mask was soon on its way. It was an extremely hot day, the sun now high overhead. I hadn't bothered with sun cream that morning, expecting to be out of the shade no longer than ten minutes. I would be burnt to a crisp in less than half an hour if I stayed out of the shade, and there was nowhere by the dock to take cover. I told Juancho that I would have to go into town to buy some sun cream, and would return as soon as I could.

"You not hurry, this fixed soon. Don't worry, not big problem. You bring us back some cold soda?"

I headed off to town, and I'd be lying if I said I didn't dawdle a bit, as I had no desire to get into the dark murky waters of the industrial port. Eventually I returned and was amazed to see half a dozen sheets of tin already drying in the sun. The mask had arrived, and Alonzo had started duck-diving in the gloomy water, feeling around with gloved hands on the bottom for the lost roof.

"How deep is it?" I asked.

"Not deep, ten, maybe twelve feet. No problem. He dive for conch and lobster much deeper than this. This easy," Juancho told me.

By now we had gathered quite a crowd of interested bystanders. Many jokes were made at our expense. However, one gringo passing by sympathised with us, saying, "I did exactly the same thing last week. Fifty sheets! Took us hours to get it all out."

"What do you want me to do?" I asked Juancho. He suggested I should just keep out of the way, and I didn't argue. Maybe I could go back to the shop and buy more soda, he added, as the first large chilled bottle had disappeared very quickly. Again I didn't protest, and could see that these two would get the job done more efficiently without another bumbling gringo in the way.

And again, perhaps I may have dawdled a little.

Paradise Delayed

When I returned Alonzo was out of the water. All the tin was laid out to dry and the guys had started loading the boat again. There were now several more ropes holding the boat in place, which now looked much less likely to tip. I joined the loading effort, and before long the boat was full. I waved the two off at the dock as the boat wallowed out into open water. Would I ever see my roof again, I wondered. Or my workers?

Of course I had underestimated Juancho's boat-handling skills. That evening, when I returned to the island, he told me the trip had been easy, the boat solid and stable on the water once moving at speed.

Alonzo was extremely pleased with the large bottle of rum I had bought for him, as a thank-you gift for his efforts above and beyond the call of duty in the grim waters at the port. He seemed none the worse for the experience, and we happily passed the rum around, laughing now at the day's adventures.

Sitting there with my team of builders in the darkness, our smiles lit by the little cooking fire, warmed by an inner glow of neat rum in the belly, I felt the first stirrings of a feeling of being at home on my little island.

Over the next few days the tin that had been in the sea got a good wash with fresh water, while the other pieces were sent up to the top of the wooden frame. It really did look like a house now. Juancho told me that it would only be a day or two until they were ready to start putting on the wood cladding that would make up the outer walls of the house.

Unfortunately, time was running out for Moe and the kids, as they would soon have to return northwards to Canada. When I had originally come down to Panama to start work at the island I had hoped to have a house somewhere near ready before they arrived. But things here progress at a Caribbean pace, everything being done on "Bocas-time". My builders had been wonderful, but earlier hold-ups had meant they hadn't started until much later than I had originally hoped. For the three month period of Moe and the kids' visit, we had rented and lived in town. Just one day before they left Juancho proudly told me, "We finished. House done!"

They had done a wonderful job, and we all celebrated that afternoon with plenty of icy cold beer brought from town. Just before dark we waved goodbye to the crew as they departed unsteadily in Juancho's boat. The island and the house were finally ours. That night we spent our first night in the new home, all sleeping suspended from the rafters in hammocks, under a roof which only a few days earlier had been on the bottom of the sea.

Lost in the mangroves

Moe and the kids had left the morning after our night in hammocks under the rafters, and I had moved to the island on a permanent basis. The lease on the little apartment in town expired at the end of the month and my couple of suitcases were easily transported by boat to my new home. Juancho and one of the other guys returned to do a couple of other jobs around the house, and I began the process of turning the empty shell into a home.

Slowly things began to take shape. With each small step forward life in the house would become a little easier and a little more comfortable. I constructed makeshift kitchen counters from off cuts of flooring or spare planks of wood. With a large second-hand 12 volt battery I had been offered in town, I set up the water pump I had brought with me to Panama. A tap in the kitchen, which produced water under pressure from the pump, seemed like absolute luxury. The same battery powered a light bulb in the main room. Light in the evening was an additional touch of modern living, although it did tend to attract many unwanted insects and moths, as I had no doors or windows.

Slowly things came together, and I thoroughly enjoyed the process of creating what, until now, I had only seen in my mind's eye. I had three months before I planned to head north, back to Whitehorse for a few months of the short summer there.

My favourite day of the week was Sunday. Almost without exception, Sunday was Rana Azul day, the biggest social gathering of the week for the residents of Dolphin Bay and the surrounding areas. I would occasionally manage a couple of hours of work on the house in the morning, before giving myself the rest of the day off.

With Janis and Bill being my nearest gringo neighbours, less than a mile away, we would often boat-pool for the twenty minute boat ride south. They lived closer to Rana Azul than I, so it made sense for me to go to their house on a Sunday morning, even if they were driving that day. To get to their house I would come out of my little bay in front of my dock, and instead of heading north to town I would head south west into the wide passage through the mangroves that leads into Dolphin Bay itself.

Bill and Janis were slightly off route, and I would detour through "the cut", a tight little passage which sliced through a narrow peninsula of mangroves, providing a handy short cut between the two properties.

Paradise Delayed

I don't know who created the cut, for it is certainly man-made, and I have asked several people if they know. I presume it was local Indian fishermen wanting to access a quicker kayuko route from Bocatorito, the little Indian village in Dolphin Bay, to Bocas Town. Or maybe it was the tour operators who run the dolphin-watching trips from Bocas down to Dolphin Bay. Whoever it was, I am always grateful. It is very narrow, just wide enough for my larger boat, which has about a foot of clearance on either side.

The first time I went through the cut I took it very slowly, idling the engine, checking the depth, and bumping from side to side as I tried to steer a straight line through the centre.

Over the following weeks I managed to negotiate the cut more confidently as my boat skills improved. Often on my way home from Rana Azul, fuelled by a few beers, I would steer through it confidently at high speed like the local taxi drivers did. I got it wrong on one occasion, bumping up onto the mangroves on the right of the boat. Fortunately this just bounced the boat back into the deeper water in the middle of the cut, and I shot out of the far end without problem. The incident did cause me to slow down a little on subsequent journeys.

The pizza restaurant is only accessible by water. Being a good distance from town, about forty minutes by boat, it tends to attract more Dolphin Bay locals than town dwellers. Sunday afternoons are always filled with laughter, interesting conversation, and as the afternoon passes, dancing too. I often think that the people who choose to make such a unique place their home tend to be pretty unique people too, and everyone there seems to have some amazing stories to tell from lives filled with challenges, fun and adventure. In many of the people there I can often see my future self, maybe twenty or thirty years from now, still living a life a little less ordinary than most, still looking for fun and adventure.

Being so far from town and from any form of authority, having a few beers and then heading for home at the helm of a boat is quite acceptable. With the bay being wide and relatively empty of traffic, it is unusual to hear of accidents. They do happen very occasionally, usually at night. In Dolphin Bay, an accident often takes the form of an unlit kayuko, the owner perhaps fishing at night, being struck by a powered boat that doesn't see him. Local-style night lights take the form of a mobile phone, screen illuminated, held high in the air for the approaching craft to see - it's not always effective, and the unfortunate fisherman may have to leap overboard before impact.

So by the end of a Sunday afternoon session Bill, Janis and I tend to be heading home in a very cheery mood. I am usually at the helm, Bill nursing a final beer for the journey - a "traveller" as they were always called when I lived in Australia - and Janis waving her arms back and forth in the air, happy in the warm twilight on the beautiful flat waters of the bay. I would laugh happily at Janis, and have often told her it is my favourite moment of the week, seeing her so happy and relaxed.

Usually I would drop them off at home and continue on my way, following the familiar maze-like journey through the mangroves to the cut, then through the wider gap back to my own bay. But on one occasion we must have departed a little earlier from Rana Azul, and approaching their house, Janis suggested a quick margarita before I continued home. Against my better judgement I agreed, and inside Bill mixed a delicious mixture, salting the rims of the glasses very professionally.

We chatted and laughed, and Bill poured the drinks again. When I thought to look out the window I was amazed to see that it was already completely dark. With Panama being only nine degrees north of the equator, night falls pretty quickly.

"May as well have another drink then," suggested Bill happily.

"I guess so," I laughed. "It can't get any darker now, can it?"

When I finally suggested it really was time for me to head home they suggested that I could stay over. However, I was confident that I'd find my way, and weaved unsteadily down their dock, armed with a big flashlight they had loaned me. I had done the journey many times in the last half-light of dusk and a couple of times at night, lit by a bright moon, but away from the bright lights of the house I realised that tonight was different. There was no moon, and it really was inky black out there. I puttered along slowly, allowing my eyes to adjust to the dark as well as they could, but the bays and inlets in the mangroves all seemed to merge into one dark black mass. It was really difficult to judge even where the water ended and the mangroves began. By now I was out of sight of the house behind me, and there was only my house ahead, unlit of course, so I had no beacon to guide me. I think I may have got a little turned around in the dark, but in my inebriated state I was still confident of my navigational ability.

It became apparent that my eyes alone were not going to be enough to get me home, and reluctantly I turned on the flashlight. Its strong beam lit up a wall of mangroves ahead, and I steered a parallel course to them, keeping them on my right.

"If I'm in the top bay," I reasoned to myself, "the cut should be just along here on the right." All mangroves look the same in the narrow beam of a flashlight, but these seemed to fit with the map I had in my head, at least for a while.

I continued to parallel the dense wall of greenery, but the cut stubbornly refused to appear. When the mangroves took a turn to the right, my mental map no longer fitted with what I could see, and I realised I didn't quite know where I was.

"Maybe I'm in the bay to the south," I reasoned, probably now talking out loud to myself. "If I cut across here I should hit the far wall, turn right and I'll be there."

I followed my own advice, cutting away from the mangroves beside me, eventually finding another impenetrable green wall where I turned right, now keeping the mangroves to my left. Again the cut didn't appear when I hoped it might. My heart sank. I was well and truly lost now. I throttled the engine back to consider my predicament. Where was I, and where had I gone wrong?

Through my slightly inebriated haze I realised that I had one huge advantage on my side - I was in a dead end bay, and couldn't fail to find my way out if I just followed a mangrove wall in one direction or another. I'd either discover the cut, or would end up back within sight of Bill and Janis's house. It looked like I might have to stay overnight with them after all. This would be much more preferable to the alternative, which was a night on the hard floor of the boat, tied to the mangroves until the sun started to rise. I certainly wouldn't be the first gringo do this, and it wasn't too big a deal really - at least it remained warm through the night, and discomfort would be the only real issue.

Expecting to find my way to the entrance of the bay more quickly by back-tracking, I turned the boat around and followed the mangroves back in the other direction. Now I was keeping them to my right again, looking for the lights of the house ahead. I was amazed when, a couple of minutes later, I found the cut through the dense undergrowth. How on earth could it be here? I was now even more confused than before.

However, I now also knew exactly where I was, and carefully made my way through the narrow gap. On the other side navigation was much easier, and I followed the mangroves on the left for a while. When they turned me to the right I headed across to the other side of the wide channel, and simply followed that side right to my little bay.

I was very relieved to fall into my own bed that night. Never again, I promised myself. My golden rule for Dolphin Bay navigation, in future, would be to always head for home before darkness falls.

Baby birds

Without doors or windows the house was open for a while to a few uninvited wild guests. At night, with a light on, insects and moths would come in, but they were never too much trouble. My most amazing moth visitor had a wingspan bigger than the spread my hand.

During the early days of May a couple of birds began flying into the house. They soon made themselves at home above the light fixture in the main room of the house. The fixture was mounted on a flat piece of wood which was screwed to two of the roof beams. Between the beams they had a perfect little nest-sized spot.

I looked them up on the internet, discovering that they were Panamanian Flycatchers, quite common to the area. They are a pretty little bird with a bright lime green breast.

For a couple of weeks they flew in and out, bringing twigs, working hard on their own construction project, while below them I worked on mine. I stood on a chair one day to have a peek in when they were both away from the house and was impressed by the size of their nest.

One day in June I was amazed to hear tiny cheeping noises from the nest. I climbed up again to look in when the two birds were away, discovering three little chicks in the nest. I hadn't even realised they already had eggs in there.

It was fascinating to watch how hard mum and dad worked to keep the little ones fed. The one I assumed to be mum was much more confident around me. She would happily come in and out, wherever I was and whatever I was doing. Even drilling and hammering didn't seem to bother her. Dad was a little bit different, lacking mum's confidence, often waiting on a tree branch outside until I was out of the way.

One evening, just as I was tidying my tools away there was a "thunk" by the newly built kitchen counter. I went to investigate, and as I approached there was a second thud. In front of me there were two wrinkled little baby birds on the hard wooden counter. They had fallen from the nest, a drop of four or five feet. They seemed to be okay, but I wasn't quite sure what to do. I remembered reading somewhere that if the babies are handled they will smell differently to the parents, who may then abandon them.

I decided to try to put them back in the nest using kitchen paper to carefully scoop them up without touching them. The operation was successful and I breathed a sigh of relief when the parents came back as darkness fell, apparently none-the-wiser.

I put a couple of thick towels down on the counter directly beneath the nest to cushion any further falls.

The next morning one of the birds was out of the nest again, having landed safely on the soft pad of towels. Again I scooped it up with kitchen towels, returning it to the nest while the adults were out hunting for food.

Over the next weeks there was a regular rain of baby birds from the nest, each returned carefully when the parents were away. I wondered if I might be doing the wrong thing. Perhaps in the wild only one baby survived? Maybe I was giving the parents an unsupportable workload?

The small, hairless, blind babies grew feathers, developing into amazingly cute copies of the parents. I often studied them before returning them to the nest, and they became quite used to having me handle them.

On a couple of occasions I had been caught red-handed by the mother bird. She seemed unconcerned about my involvement, patiently waiting as I returned a baby to the nest. I was no longer bothering to use kitchen towels to pick up the fallen chicks, and there had been no rejection. I think the mother now accepted me as part of the parental process.

She returned to the nest one day, just as a baby tumbled to the kitchen counter. I was sitting nearby, watching to see what she would do. She flew down to the kitchen counter, looked at the little baby there, then looked at me. I know I shouldn't anthropomorphise, but her look really did communicate a simple message. "You're going to have to help me with this," was my mental translation. She watched calmly as I returned the baby to the nest.

One of the little ones had become very tame, happy to sit on my finger as I wandered around the house. Unfortunately, one night, as I returned it to the nest, it fell and, trying to flap its wings, missed the towel pad. It banged the edge of the counter hard, tumbling to the floor. It looked very stunned as I carefully replaced it again.

I was very sad to find it in the nest the next morning, cold and stiff. The other two were still doing well, however, and a couple of days later the initial flights began.

The babies would leap from the nest and flap frantically, slowly gaining ability to control their flight, but still quite clumsy. I returned from feeding the chickens one morning, confused to find there was only one small bird left in the house. Mum and dad were on the tree outside, chirping encouragement. Perhaps the first one had already left? But I could hear two separate little chirps of reply, so went hunting for second one.

The plaintive little peeps were coming from inside the wall by the front door. I was only halfway through boarding the inside walls. Perhaps the little bird had tried to land on the top board and then fallen down the narrow gap between the outer and inner wall. It took a while to strip off enough boards to be able to effect a rescue.

Later that morning, as I replaced the boards, the babies departed with their parents, landing in bushes near the front of the house. I wished them well, sad to see them go, but proud of the small part I had played in the parental process.

Now, almost a year later, I occasionally see a Panama Flycatcher in one of the trees on the island. I wonder if it is one of the babies that shared my house for a while. Perhaps it will be looking for a nest site soon to raise its own babies. I leave the back door invitingly open each day.

Border crossings

Now let's get one thing clear at the outset here - I'm not advocating that a full time career as a professional document forger should be anyone's next career move, but on occasion it does help if you can get a little creative with the paperwork.

These days international travel can be fraught with difficulties, especially since events in New York in 2001 and the subsequent tightening of controls in both the States and elsewhere.

But in the last couple of years I have come upon an increasingly troublesome regulation. I came across this for the first time in 2010, but seem to have run up against this time and again since then.

Maybe it is because my travel isn't quite so structured and organised as it was when I tackled my 100 goals over a two year period. Maybe regulations have changed.

The problem I keep running into is the apparent need for proof of onward travel from some countries, before entrance will be granted. I first came across this in 2010, as Moe and I headed down to Panama by bus from Costa Rica. At the border everybody was being asked by Panamanian officials for some sort of proof that they had travel plans that eventually took them out of the country.

Moe and I had copies of our flight details back out of San Jose, and this seemed to be acceptable. Others, less fortunate, had to pay out $20 to the driver of our bus for a hand written return bus ticket. Once passports had been stamped, the bus driver kindly offered to buy the tickets back and sell them on to other travellers who might actually get to use them. The buy-back price was only $10. Welcome to Central American travel.

On subsequent border crossings I have had my proof of a booking for a flight departing from San Jose refused, and have had to buy a bus ticket myself. Fortunately it was one valid for a year, and I did eventually use it.

On my third crossing I became a little more creative. Not that I am suggesting that you should try this, but with a little work on Photoshop it is easy to take a previous booking, change a date or two, even the departure airport and price you paid. When this is printed out, folded and re-folded a couple of times, and a circular coffee mug stain added to it, the result is a very convincing document showing apparent proof of onward travel.

Border crossings

In Central America the border officials only ever seem to make a quick visual check of any paperwork you offer, and no details seem to be input into a computer - believe me, I've watched closely.

However, I have come upon this problem a few times more recently too, and not just in Central America.

This onward travel requirement now seems to be being applied in such a hap-hazard fashion the world over. I have now had some very difficult flight departures and immigration arrivals.

It seems that to travel freely, without plans set in concrete and a pre-booked itinerary, is now considered to be unusual, and is highly discouraged.

Here are just a couple of examples... I have many others.

In 2011, flying from London to San Jose in Costa Rica, I was stopped at the check-in desk by an overly efficient desk clerk. My journey would take me first to Florida, then down to Costa Rica from there. My flights were with different airlines, so the agent only had details of my flight into Miami. Did I have onward travel from the States booked, she wanted to know, and could she see my ticket?

Certainly. I pulled my small laptop out of my hand luggage and booted it up. It's an old computer, and has travelled the world with me for over three years now, so is a little slow to get started, but the agent waited patiently.

Finally I managed to open my email software, and showed her the flight confirmation email for my Fort Lauderdale to San Jose flight, booked for a few days later.

"Okay," she smiled. "I'll just need a print-out of that."

"Sorry? I don't have a print of this. I've never needed a print-out before."

"Well I need a copy. That's our policy."

"Whose policy?"

"The airline. We can be fined if you don't exit the country within your allotted time on your visa and we didn't check your exit details."

I had a couple of hours before my flight was due to depart, so wasn't unduly concerned. I tried to argue my case. I had the details on my computer there in front of us. I had nowhere to print out the document. What if I was staying in the States for a while longer, and hadn't yet

Paradise Delayed

booked a flight out? What if I planned to head out of the States overland, maybe by bus, or even by boat?

She had answers for everything. There were computers upstairs where I could print out my tickets. If I was leaving the US by bus, she'd need to see my ticket, which I would have had to book in advance. Or a boat ticket.

"Doesn't leave much room for travelling flexibility, does it?" I pointed out.

"Sorry sir, I don't make the rules."

I obviously wasn't getting anywhere, and dragged my luggage upstairs in search of a printer connected to a computer. I found a couple of coin-in-the-slot computers, one of which offered print options. I put a pound in the slot, but when I signed into my email online, I realised the email I wanted wasn't be there. My email program on my computer is set to download email from the server, then delete it from the server inbox, which prevents me hitting inbox size limits.

The document wasn't available online, and there was no way to connect my computer to the printer. What to do?

Ah-ha! Maybe I could forward the email to myself from my computer, then print it off from the web before I ran another send/receive with my email software. Brilliant!

I'd have to hurry, as my pound only bought me a few minutes of internet time on the airport computer. I started the process of coaxing my laptop out of hibernation once again.

I looked for an airport wi-fi connection, only to discover that the airport didn't offer free wi-fi. Surely, in this day and age, a free wi-fi connection should be a basic provision at any airport. But no! It was going to cost me five pounds for 24 hours of internet access.

As I stared at this in despair, my original pound ran out in the machine, and it returned to its default advertising screen.

None of the teenage staff at any of the fast food outlets nearby could suggest any other place where I might be able to get something printed.

That's it, I fumed. I headed back downstairs to confront the desk clerk once again, and found that now the queue to check-in had got larger. I joined the line, hoping that I might get a different counter, thereby avoiding the obstructive lady who had previously dealt with me.

I did get a different clerk this time, but he was right next to the unhelpful lady's desk. Before I had got halfway through my story of email challenges, she leaned over, and explained that she had already told me that I couldn't be checked in without a print-out of my onward ticket.

I looked hopefully at the new clerk, but he shrugged his shoulders in what looked to be a slightly sympathetic manner, and suggested that the Customer Service desk may be able to help me. I joined the short queue there, hopping from foot to foot, as departure time, and more importantly, last check-in time, were now looming a little closer.

When my turn came I explained the situation, and asked if they had a printer. They didn't, and did not have any helpful suggestions. I asked to speak to the manager. I explained my predicament to her, and asked why they need a print-out.

Could I show her my booking, she asked me? I fired up my computer again. Once I pulled up my email, she looked at it and asked, "You do have travel booked onward from Costa Rica, don't you?"

"Well, I'll be travelling down to Panama by bus from San Jose, and I'll be staying there for a few months," I explained. "With a friend," I added lamely. I thought that mentioning that I owned property in Panama would only serve to further cloud the already murky waters.

"The problem is that you have to have proof of onward travel out of America," she said helpfully.

"I do. To Costa Rica."

"No… onward out of the contiguous United States."

"Sorry? What do you mean?" I was truly flummoxed now.

"You have to have proof of travel out of any country contiguous with the USA."

"I do. To Costa Rica," I repeated, sounding a little foolish. "There are several other countries between the USA and Costa Rica, including Mexico."

"No, the US counts all of them as contiguous," she proclaimed.

"They don't!" I splurted. I was aware now of time slipping away.

"Well," she pronounced. "We'll just have to ask a US Border protection representative."

She made a phone call, despite my protests that I was about to miss my flight, and to my surprise a lady in a US uniform appeared very quickly.

Paradise Delayed

"What seems to be the problem?" she drawled. I remained quiet and let the customer service rep dig her own hole. Once the US border lady had a grasp of the issues she carefully explained that Costa Rica wasn't contiguous with the USA. If I had a ticket to San Jose, and duly used it, I would be of no further interest to US Border Protection. "Do you have an onward ticket, sir? She asked me.

I turned my computer around to show her. "Let the man get on his flight," she suggested, and walked off.

I had the embarrassed customer service rep accompany me to the original check-in desk, where we skipped the line. "But he doesn't have a print-out..." she began.

"Just check him in or he'll miss this flight." I had made check-in with a minute or two to spare, and caught the flight without having to have a print-out of my proof of onward travel.

Despite the fact that I had lost two hours of waiting room reading time, I felt like I had won a small victory.

My second example took place just over a year later, entering Canada at Toronto. I was flying up from Florida, heading ultimately for Whitehorse on the other side of the country. I had had previous issues entering Canada before without an exit flight booked, and on that occasion, as I was planning on staying almost the full six months that the visitor's visa would grant me, I had had many questions to answer.

Their main concern had been that I had sufficient finances in place to fund a six month visit without resort to either work, or financial assistance from the Canadian welfare system. I managed to convince the border agent that I had sufficient funds, and she suggested that next time I bring along a print-out of my bank statement to prove my solvency. I promised I would.

So approaching the desk in Toronto I foresaw no problems, as I had a copy of a recent bank statement ready to whip out when the opportunity presented itself.

"When do you fly out of Canada?" the Toronto agent asked me.

"In about two months," I answered brightly.

"Can I see your ticket?"

"Ah, I haven't booked one yet, as I'm not sure of exact dates. I do have a print-out of my bank statement," I added helpfully.

"I don't need to see your bank statement; I need to see proof of onward travel." I heaved a heavy sigh, which I don't think particularly endeared me to the stern-faced lady. Here we go again, I thought.

"Last time..." I began. I explained how it had been suggested that a bank statement would be enough to brighten any border agent's day, and smooth my entry to the northern latitudes. It obviously wasn't going to be the case today.

I had about four hours until my connecting flight, and settled in for a long discussion. "What if I end up driving back down to the States?"

"I'd need to see a car hire agreement."

"With a friend? In her car? How could I prove that?"

"I'd still want to see a flight booked out of the country before I let you in."

"Why?" I asked reasonably. "That would be such a waste of money if I never used it. I can book a flight at any time, and will do so when plans become a little firmer. Why should I have to have a flight booked now?"

"Because that's what I need to see."

"Look at my passport," I suggested, my frustration perhaps beginning to show a little. "You can see that I travel a lot. I have no intention, or desire for that matter, to stay longer than a couple of months of the summer. I have been in and out of Canada several times in the past few years. I have never once overstayed my visa. I have never been in trouble with the law, worked, or otherwise given the Canadian authorities any cause for concern. Why should I now be facing such obstacles to return?"

"Because you need to have proof of onward travel."

"I never have needed it before."

"Well, you need it today."

We parried back and forth for a while, her suggesting that she could refuse to let me in if she chose to do so, and me suggesting that as I didn't currently have a flight booked, and couldn't fix that right now, she would just have to accept my bank statement as proof of onward travel plans.

She eventually relented and gave me a six month visitor's visa, telling me that my name would be "red flagged".

"What does that mean? Why should I be red flagged just because my travel plans don't fit the regular two-week-holiday mould?"

Paradise Delayed

"Just don't come back to Canada again without an onward ticket booked, because you will be turned back at the border," she told me sternly.

"Really?" I don't know if she "red flagged" me or not, but what a welcome to a country for a visitor coming to spend time and money.

You'd think I would have learned my lesson by then, wouldn't you. I'd never had any problems before when flying down to Costa Rica from the States. At the end of my two month stay in Canada I flew to LA, entering the US without a hitch. I had an onward ticket from LA to Florida, and from there down to San Jose once again.

For the first time ever, in many departures from the US, at LAX airport the check-in desk clerk wanted to see proof of onward travel from Costa Rica. I was amazed. I asked the usual questions, and received the usual answers... airline policy... we don't make the rules... just doing my job.

I explained that I would be catching the bus from San Jose to Bocas del Toro, where I planned to stay for about six months.

"I'll need to see a bus ticket then."

"They don't exactly sell them online - it's a bit of a local chicken bus. I don't even know if they have a website."

"Well, I'm sorry, but I'm not checking you in this evening without an onward ticket of some sort." It was now about 8pm, and my red-eye to Florida departed at 10.

I headed back upstairs to the food hall and found a seat. I fired up the computer and tried to find a way to book a bus ticket online. I found the website for the bus journey I planned on making, but it merely showed rudimentary timetable information. There was a telephone number, however, and I was amazed when someone answered it.

In my halting Spanish I tried to explain that I needed to buy a ticket, and needed an email confirming my purchase. Call in the morning was the response, as best as I could understand it - the boss will be in then. I think I had been talking to the office cleaner.

Okay, what about a flight? I switched on Skype and was very lucky to find Moe online. She was planning to head down to Panama again with her kids to avoid the worst of the chilly Canadian winter. I had six weeks on my own on the island to get the place ready to house a family of four. When they arrived they would be there for three and a half months. Maybe if I booked a ticket back to Florida at the same time as they were leaving, we could all travel north together. I didn't really have any further plans when they left.

Moe gave me her travel dates, and I got online to look at departures from San Jose around the same time as the three of them. Maybe I could continue northwards at the end of February with them and visit their family in Montreal.

We made some loose plans quickly, and online I found a great flight with the airline with which I was about to travel south. It was cheap, and on the same day as Moe and the kids' homeward flight. I went ahead and booked it, returning downstairs triumphantly to check in with ten minutes to spare.

"Oh no sir, this flight won't do. You have to exit the country within 90 days of entering. The flight you have booked is five months after entry."

"Yes, I understand that," I said through gritted teeth, "but I'll be travelling down to Panama. They give six month tourist visas. I'll then come back up into Costa Rica."

"In that case I'll need to see a bus ticket."

Back to Square One.

"Okay. How about this? It's now 9pm, and there is no way I can get a bus ticket online until tomorrow. Let me get on the flight from here to Florida. I'll be there from 5am to 10am before the San Jose flight leaves. I'll be able to book a bus ticket then. That'll work, won't it?"

I'm sorry sir, but the two flights were booked as one journey, so I have to issue both boarding passes. I can't do that without seeing a ticket for onward travel."

Arrgghh! "But I could have booked the flights as two separate legs. The cost on your website would have been exactly the same. If I hadn't told you about the second flight I'd be checked-in for Florida by now."

"Yes, but you didn't book them separately, I do know of your onward plans, so you are not checked-in yet."

I had one final possibility, which Moe had suggested. I was somewhat reluctant, but I had five minutes left before I missed this flight and lost my money.

"Okay. What if I book a flight right now that comes back from Costa Rica within the next three months?" A full price, fully refundable ticket was to be my last desperate gamble. I had checked out the terms and

Paradise Delayed

conditions while researching other flights upstairs, and was reasonably confident I would get my money back.

"Yes, that would be fine," I was told. I was then asked to move aside for the final couple of customers waiting to check-in.

The internet connection signal showed as "very weak" and the airline website seemed to take forever to load pages. I finally managed to pay the exorbitant price of $650 for a one way from San Jose to Miami, picked for a random date about two months away.

I spun the computer round triumphantly as the confirmation page slowly loaded, and breathed a sigh of relief as I was finally checked-in a couple of minutes late.

The line for security scanning was long, which meant I had to run to arrive at the gate just as boarding started. Another close scrape.

On the flight down to San Jose I mocked up a ticket from Panama City to Miami, and had it printed out at one of the many internet shops in the city centre. At the Panamanian border I had no trouble getting in, receiving the usual six months visitor's visa.

A week later I managed to get my $650 fully refunded too.

Fully refundable tickets, or blatant forgery - the choice is yours if you want to travel without the restrictions of a set itinerary. Welcome to 21st Century travel.

Cameron's trip home

Before heading off to Canada for the summer I needed to find someone to look after the property, so I put the word out with the regulars at Rana Azul. My friends Steve and Jeanne, long term Bocas house-sitters, would have been my first choice, but they already had other commitments. I sent out an email to my large contact list, outlining what I was looking for and the responsibilities entailed. Basically, all someone needed to do, to look after my place, was to feed the chickens once a day and make sure the termites didn't get a foothold in the house.

There was a great deal of response from my mailing list of friends and contacts, but much of it was expressing regrets. Not many people, it would appear, can take three months out of their schedule to go and lounge around on a private Caribbean island.

I had a few offers of a month here and a month there, but I held out for someone who could do the whole three months. With the home being off-grid and the lifestyle being slightly unusual, I was keen to be able to pass on my instruction to the house-sitter personally. If there was a succession of three or four people looking after the place, these details would have to be passed on in a complicated form of Chinese whispers, and I imagined it wouldn't be long before the propeller was clattered off my engine on some shallow outcropping of coral.

Ryan, a good friend in Australia, put the word around. He eventually introduced me via email to Cameron, another Aussie currently working in London, completing his training to be a lawyer.

We discussed dates and options, eventually deciding we could make it work if I came back from Canada a week earlier than I had originally planned. Cameron hadn't handled a boat before, but had lived in the outback of Australia for a while, he told me. A few people warned against having a house-sitter without boat handling experience, but I didn't really have any other viable option, so Cameron got the job.

I met him at the airport when he flew in, and we dropped his bag off at Mark's real estate office in town just a few blocks away. I was keen to introduce him to Mark, who had offered to help him out with any town-based issues he had over the next three months. After showing Cameron a few of the useful locations in town - shops, laundry and bars - we loaded the boat and headed for the island.

Over the next day and a half I showed Cameron how everything worked. I gave him a very condensed boat-handling course, pointing out the reefs

Paradise Delayed

to avoid at the entrance to my bay. He appeared to pick everything up pretty quickly, and I was pretty confident he wouldn't have too many problems. We went around the corner to visit Bill and Janis, who also promised to look after him. "Oh, he's very handsome, isn't he?" grinned Janis, winking at me. There was obviously going to be some dancing at Rana Azul in Cameron's near future. We arranged for him to go with them to the restaurant that weekend.

The following morning Cameron took me to town in *Ay Caramba*, my little boat which I was now using almost all the time. It was much cheaper on fuel and was ideal for one or two people. He dropped me off at the water taxi dock where we shook hands.

"Thanks for this opportunity," he said. "Have a great trip. Now, just point me in the right direction for the island again." He grinned, and I was unsure if he was joking, but I carefully pointed him in the right direction. As the water taxi left town I hoped he would make it back home again.

As always, when you leave something behind in someone else's hands, the last days had been a bit frantic. I hoped that I had told Cameron everything he needed to know. However, as various forms of transport took me further north, the island seemed further and further away. By the time I got to Whitehorse, met at the airport by Moe and the kids, Panama was pushed away to the back of my thoughts.

I only spoke to Cameron a couple of times over the next three months, having jokingly told him he didn't need to contact me with any small issues. I didn't want to know if anything broke, or stopped working.

"Just fix it and I'll reimburse anything you have to spend when I get back. Only contact me if the place burns to the ground," I had told him before I left.

My house didn't burn to the ground, and three months later I returned to find everything in much the same condition in which I had left it. It appeared that Cameron wasn't too much of a handyman, as I had a couple of sink drains to fix. However, he had built a couple of extra facilities for the chickens in my absence.

We had collected a case of beer in town when he had picked me up and that night, as we sat on the balcony he told me of many of his experiences from the past months - some of them funny, some slightly alarming.

Left on his own after I departed, he said he had wondered what he had let himself in for. He had enjoyed the first trip out to Rana Azul, happy to meet the friendly group of neighbours, but on the way home had asked Janis a question.

"That was great fun," he had said. "What are we doing tomorrow?"

Janis told me later that he had looked very crestfallen when she explained that that was pretty-much it until next week. She had taken pity on him and invited him around for dinner later in the week. Cameron told me that in that first week he had really been quite down, thinking that the three months ahead looked long and lonely.

But once he got to know a few people his social circle expanded, and he met a few younger people who were travelling on sailboats and were in town for a while. When Bill and Janis headed back to the States for a while they had an attractive younger female house-sitter look after their place, and Cameron decided that he had landed on his feet.

Cameron was a single guy, and his three month stay at my house had coincided with an influx of younger female visitors to the area. From what Cameron told me, and from stories I heard from others later, Cameron had become known as a bit of a tom cat around Dolphin Bay.

He only had one major disaster in his three month tenure of the island, when he managed to sink poor little *Ay Caramba*. Again, gleaning information from both Cameron, and later from other sources, he had been quite drunk at the time, and had an even drunker female companion with him. She had stood up in the little boat and stepped towards the back, by the engine, to join Cameron on the seat there. The boat is small, and the 25 horsepower engine on the back is really too big for it - it does go fast though! With the combined weight of the engine and two people at the back, the stern dipped under the surface of the water, and the little boat filled rapidly. It had simply sunk to the bottom from underneath the hapless pair. Fortunately the engine hadn't been running, and Cameron got it to Mario, the local mechanic, pretty quickly. Before I returned to Bocas the engine was back on the boat, and all was well again with *Ay Caramba*.

I asked him if he had enjoyed his time here, wondering what he had thought of the three months spent in this place.

"It's been life-changing," he answered. "No seriously. There really is something special about this place. Not just the place though; it's the people, the weather, the lifestyle. I love it. It really has made me think about how I want to live the rest of my life and where I want to go from here. I'm very jealous of what you have here, Ian, and I'm eternally grateful for the opportunity you have offered me."

Paradise Delayed

"Wow, I'm very flattered, and happy you enjoyed yourself. I'm just glad both my boats are still floating and all the chickens are alive," I laughed.

The next day was Sunday, Cameron's last in Bocas. He had issued invites to all and sundry to come to Rana Azul to share a last afternoon there with him. We headed down in the little boat, arriving at noon before most of the others. Lyn was already there, as she usually is, and it was good to see her again. She lives to the north of me and passes my dock on the way to Rana Azul, usually beating me there, as she gets a good early start.

As others arrived I enjoyed catching up with old friends I had missed over the summer. I got a glimpse of how well Cameron had fitted in over his three month visit. A lot of people had become very fond of him, and he was going to be very much missed. Each well-wisher bought him a drink, and as the afternoon progressed it was obvious that I was going to be driving the boat home.

As people began to leave later in the afternoon I circulated back around to where Cameron was chatting with a small group of people. By now he had had so many drinks bought for him he was only semi-coherent. Swaying slightly, and occasionally staggering, he needed support from one of the group around him. Oh dear. I wandered off to chat to someone else and left him to it.

A little later I turned around to see Cameron sprawled on the floor. I assumed he had taken a drunken tumble. He didn't appear hurt, and was climbing slowly to his feet. Only later did I find out from Lyn that he had received a very firm knee to the groin from Molly. Months later I found out from Molly herself that she too had been very drunk, and the next morning said blearily to her husband that she thought she may have kneed someone the day before. I asked Cameron later how he had caused offence, but could get no sense out of him, so have no idea what he said to Molly to provoke the response. To this day neither does Molly. I guess it will be forever a mystery.

Time to leave, I thought, and went to collect Cameron. There were only a few people left, and we said some final goodbyes as I steered Cameron down the dock and into the little boat. I gave the fuel line a bit of a squeeze and pulled the starter cord. Nothing. I tried a few times, but couldn't get the engine to start. Before I had left I knew exactly how to get the engine to fire, but seemed to have lost my knack.

"Here, I'll do it," slurred Cameron, standing up and heading my way. I had to move quickly to avert a second sinking, swapping places with Cameron. He almost went overboard on the first pull, and through my laughter I suggested he should sit down. He was having none of it, and tried again as a small crowd of others heading home paused to watch the show.

I eventually managed to get Cameron to sit down again, and tried once more with the engine. By now everyone except Lyn and Molly had left, perhaps slightly disappointed not to see Cameron take a swim.

"Come on Ian, I'll tow you home," offered Lyn, and I gratefully accepted. It was getting late and we quickly sorted out ropes, tying *Ay Caramba* firmly to the stern of Lyn's powerful boat on a long line.

Casting off from the dock, Lyn took up the slack. She drove slowly at first then, as we reached open water, she tried to speed up. However, with both Cameron and I in the little boat it dragged heavily, and we were in danger of snapping the rope. We continued like this for a while, but darkness was coming, and we really needed to pick up some speed. Lyn throttled back and I hauled us alongside with the rope. We decided it would be much better if I got in Lyn's bigger boat, making the smaller one much lighter to tow. Cameron was by now fast asleep, curled up in the front of the little boat.

"Just leave him there," said Lyn laughing. "He'll be fine."

Once on the move again the little boat towed well, soon lifting up onto the plane, skipping along behind us. Keen to get home before dark, Lyn pushed the throttle a little further. As we speeded up the wake from her boat lengthened and narrowed, leaving only a small space between the twin waves for the small boat. It skittered from side to side a little, but seemed pretty stable. There was no sign of life from Cameron in the bottom of the boat. As we turned slightly to the right to enter the wide passage between Tierra Oscura and Dolphin Bay, I looked back to see how things were going behind. I watched in horror as my little boat climbed the wake on the starboard side, suddenly dropping over it. I have no idea how it didn't flip, and imagined it would certainly have done so without Cameron's weight in the bottom stabilising it.

"Better slow down a bit, I guess?" Lyn drawled through a big smile. "Don't want to lose him, do we?"

"I don't care if we do," slurred Molly cheerily. "Cheeky little bastard!" she laughed, in obvious reference to whatever had been said earlier.

"I do care about my boat though. Let's not sink it again," I offered, as Lyn slowed ever so slightly. As we continued north through Dolphin Bay at a good pace I mentally prepared to leap overboard to grab the comatose Cameron if we did flip the little boat. However, Lyn had

Paradise Delayed

everything under control, slowing carefully before we entered the mangroves just before we got to my bay.

"Just untie us here, offshore," I told her. "Lend me that paddle and I'll row us in from here." The reef across the front of my bay meant that Lyn would have to go the long way round to get into the dock, whereas my little boat could easily enter where it was shallower. I clambered in over the still sleeping Cameron, said my thanks and goodbyes, telling them to hurry before the last of the light faded.

I tied the boat at the dock, and after much tapping and cajoling got Cameron up and moving. Getting him onto the dock was fraught with danger, and I feared he may pull us both in as I helped him up. I steered him along the dock, and safely on dry land we made our way to the house, Cameron stumbling and falling a couple of times.

Back at the house he seemed to gain a new lease of life, insisting on more beer. "Let's get really drunk," he suggested, in obvious denial of the fact that he already was.

I humoured him, at one point having to suggest that he not sit on the balcony handrail, as he had swayed backwards and I had to leap forward and grab him to prevent him toppling over. It was a drop of twelve feet onto a pretty solid surface below.

We played music, and I tried some conversation, but only had limited success. Eventually I lay on the sofa, a bit tipsy myself. I closed my eyes, hoping Cameron might be inspired by my actions. Things seemed to go quiet, and I lay still for a further ten minutes. I found Cameron fast asleep half in the kitchen and half on the rear balcony, beer still clutched in his hand. I took the beer and poured it down the sink, threw a towel over him, and went to bed.

The next morning, when my alarm woke me at 6am, Cameron was already up and about, packing his bags and making some breakfast.

"How are you this morning?" I asked blearily.

"Hey, g'day mate! Great. Slept sound. Woke up in the kitchen. How did we get home last night?" he asked, perhaps suggesting that waking somewhere other than his own bed wasn't an entirely uncommon experience.

We ate quickly, and at the dock Cameron managed to start the boat on the second pull of the starter cord. I was going to have to re-learn the engine's finicky starting requirements.

Cameron's trip home

In town, at the water taxi dock, we said our goodbyes as we had three months earlier. This time Cameron was leaving and I was heading back to my island. As I climbed back down into the little boat he grinned and asked, "Do you want me to point you in the right direction?"

The Bocas Net

Bocas has a big sailing community, the little archipelago being a popular destination with many cruising couples and live-aboard families. There are several marinas in the area catering to the sailing fraternity, and endless possibilities for anchoring freely in a beautiful secluded lagoon. Some sailors end up staying in the archipelago for months on end, attracted and then kept here by the beautiful surroundings and relatively benign weather. Bocas is located just south of the hurricane belt. As hurricane season approaches in the tropical North Atlantic in June, boats in large numbers make their way here to avoid the potential for dangerous weather conditions further to the north

Several long-term cruisers have eventually decided to make Bocas their home, setting anchor here on a more permanent basis. Some have even bought land and once again becoming "dirt dwellers". With such a unique crossover into the local community, the Bocas Net was inevitable.

Sailors use a VHF radio network to keep in touch with each other, using this for general communication and emergencies too. A VHF handset is relatively inexpensive and, depending on the size of aerial used and the surrounding terrain, can receive and transmit over pretty good distances.

I first heard about the BEN network from Eric. He knew that people living in the area used marine radios to keep in touch with each other, but had no further info, as he lived in town on the main island and had no need for such communication. He could pick up a cell phone signal at any time in town, but for residents in the bays to the south of Bocas, mobile phone coverage is patchy at best.

On one of my early visits to Rana Azul I was introduced to Captain Ron, an ex-sailor now living in the archipelago.

"We need to get you a radio Ian," he informed me. "You are right in the middle of the archipelago. With a decent aerial you'll be able to get out to everyone. We'll have you running the Net one morning."

"Er, right." I wasn't quite sure what he was talking about, but he was very enthusiastic. Before the afternoon was out he had introduced me to Doctor Mark, who had a radio to sell. I became the newest member of The Bocas Net.

"You'll need a BEN number," Brent told me. Captain Ron had steered me over to meet a friendly Canadian guy who was in charge of BEN numbers, whatever they were. "I'll email you a list of everyone on the net. You can pick a number that isn't being used."

"Er, right," I answered again. I eventually discovered that BEN is an acronym for Bocas Emergency Network, and that each householder with a radio has a BEN number. My birth year was available, and I became BEN 63.

The radio I had purchased from Doctor Mark didn't come with an aerial, but my neighbour Bill came to the rescue, offering me the small aerial from his little boat.

"The radio in the boat doesn't work at the moment," he told me, "so you may as well take it and use it for now." As we removed it from the boat, pulling the cable out of the channel it ran through in the hull of the boat, we pulled a thin piece of rope through the conduit to make returning the aerial cable in future an easy task.

At my house I connected the radio to my 12 volt system and ran the aerial cable along the side of the house, the aerial attached as high as possible. The signal was great, and I could hear people from all over the archipelago, as well as most of the boats in the marinas to the north.

My first call was to Bill, BEN 42, to tell him I was up and running, and to thank him for the loan of the aerial. The call is supposed to be made in a standardised way according to marine conventions, and land-based users follow the same conventions. "BEN 4-2, BEN 4-2, BEN 4-2, this is BEN 6-3." Once communication is established on the contact channel, Channel 68, the two parties can pick a different channel to move to for their conversation, leaving the contact channel free and clear for the next call-up.

My next call was to Captain Ron, who was still keen to get me "running the Net one morning". I was pleased that he thought it best to wait until I got a better aerial, as I still only had a vague idea of what he was talking about.

The next morning at quarter to eight, or "zero-seven-forty-five" in radio parlance, I listened in to my first Bocas Net. Captain Ron was the net controller that morning, and both residents and cruisers checked in to take part in the lively morning discussion. Topics covered included any emergency issues, community announcements, boat problems, and an eclectic open forum session at the end. With VHF radios only being able to either transmit or to receive at any one time, unlike a telephone where both people can speak at once, it is important to ensure that only one person is speaking at a time. That is where the net controller comes in, ensuring that radio traffic is orderly and people aren't talking over the top of each other.

Paradise Delayed

Each day a different controller would be in charge of the net, each with their own style and way of doing things, but generally following the same format. Having used two-way radios, when driving dump trucks in the mines I had worked in when I'd lived in Australia, the system was pretty familiar. When the larger aerial I had ordered finally arrived I was keen and ready to take a spot as controller one morning.

Once I got the hang of it and after a few swap-arounds, as people came and went from the archipelago, I ended up with a regular Monday morning slot. This didn't exactly suit me, as I would occasionally feel a little under the weather after a long afternoon at Rana Azul the day before. Captain Ron kept promising to swap me to another day, but I don't think the Monday morning slot is very popular with others either, probably for similar reasons. I was still doing Mondays by the time Cameron came to house-sit.

He was quickly encouraged to fill my place when I headed up to Canada. Very soon, from what I heard later, he became a very popular morning controller, writing poems and putting his own unique Aussie twist on his broadcast. He was a bit of a tough act to follow when I returned, many people telling me that they missed Cameron's accent and poetry.

But if I thought that Cameron was a hard act to follow, I had an even bigger challenge ahead. When Moe and the kids came down that winter Maible was intrigued by the radio, and keen to use it to chat to others. She's only nine years old, but very confident and outgoing. After listening to my Monday morning broadcast the first week she was there, she asked me if she could maybe have a try one day.

"Absolutely," I answered, thinking she would never actually do it.

For the next week she read and re-read the outline script that Ron had initially given me before my first effort. She re-wrote it to suit herself, practicing it over and over. By the time the next week came around she was ready. I had mentioned to a few people at Rana Azul on Sunday that there might be a guest controller running the Net the next day.

I did the initial welcome, introduced Maible, and handed the microphone over to her. She did a marvellous job, and I hovered behind her to help with anything she might struggle with. At the end of the broadcast there were many calls of congratulations, and Maible looked justifiably proud. The following week she was keen to do it again. This time she needed no introduction. At Rana Azul she had been complimented many times, told far too often for my liking, "So much better than Ian does it."!!

By the third or fourth week she was flying completely solo, and I could go about my morning routine, just keeping half an ear on the proceedings. She was confident, chatty, and obviously popular. "It's like seeing a little baby bird fly from the nest," I said to Moe proudly.

At Rana Azul in the following weeks, or wherever I would meet newly arrived cruisers, I would be asked what my call sign was on the radio. When I told them I was BEN 63, the response was always similar. "Ahh, you must be Maible's dad? She's very good, isn't she?" In fact, at times Maible was often asked where her older sister was today, many newcomers not believing that the little girl they had just met was the one they had heard on the radio earlier in the week.

When their three and a half month stay at the island came to an end, I planned to head out with them. We would travel up to Canada together, then I planned to travel onward to England for a while. But it was Maible on the net that everyone was going to miss. How do I fill those big shoes when I return? As I write this I have yet to face that issue.

However, I did get a small role to play, despite Maible's strong takeover bid, when Captain Ron, who usually does the daily weather report, informed us one morning that his internet connection was down. He wouldn't be making his daily predictions, as he couldn't gather the information he needed. I called him after the morning net, telling him that I was supplied by a different internet provider, my connection being via one of the cell phone networks. I often still had coverage when he didn't. Maybe if he sent me a list of the websites he gathered his information from, I could step in to help out on the days he had problems?

Ron was very keen on the idea and quickly sent me a list of websites with some detailed instructions. Before I knew it he had me doing weather reports three mornings a week!

The main reason for the network to exist is, as the name Bocas Emergency Net would suggest, to offer communications in emergency situations. With our little community being spread out over quite an area, and with cell phone cover or internet unavailable in some of the more remote areas, it is vital to have a reliable means of calling for assistance. But thankfully emergencies are few and far between, and the radio network is generally used as more of a social hub for a scattered community. All sorts of social gatherings and personal arrangements are organised over the net.

On occasion there is an emergency, but it is often something simply solved - perhaps a boat engine that has failed out in the bay, and a neighbour needed to come and tow the hapless resident. On one stormy night I overheard discussions between boats in the open water anchorage.

Paradise Delayed

They were calmly discussing how to avoid tragedy as one boat's anchor dragged across the sand, making a serious collision a possibility.

Sadly, one evening I overheard an emotional series of calls. One resident's wife had suffered a heart attack, and he was in the process of administering CPR. She had been without a pulse for some time, and it was heart-wrenching to hear the doctor say that by the time someone could get to his remote location, there would be no chance of reviving her at all. The decision was made that at night it would be risking further lives to make the fruitless journey, and my heart went out to a man who had a long lonely night ahead of him.

The incident really did bring home to me the fact that I was living in a retirement community, and that for many of the people here, this was where they had chosen to come and live out the latter part of their lives. This sad loss of a friend and neighbour was not the first time this had happened, and it certainly wouldn't be the last.

But more than balancing the sad occasions, there is much amusement to be had from living among a more elderly group, especially when they all have to communicate by radio. With so many being of more advanced years, in many cases their hearing isn't what it once was. In person at Rana Azul, or at other social gatherings, this simply results in louder conversations, but on the radio the mis-communication can be comedic.

These conversations can be further complicated and confused when one of the callers has poor reception. Often a middleman is needed to relay the information between the two parties. Usually I try to steer clear of such confusion.

One person may put out a call to, for example, BEN 35, calling their station three times. When 35 responds his reply isn't heard by the original caller, who calls again. Someone else will jump in, shouting, "He's answering you, Rita," followed again by the second party who is trying to respond to the call.

Silence will fall for a second or two, and then another voice will say, "Was someone calling BEN 25?"

Oven relocation

With only six weeks between my return to relieve Cameron of his house-sitting duties, and Moe, Finn and Maible's projected arrival in November, I had my work cut out. There was a long list of jobs that needed completing to make the house habitable for a family of four. Things had been pretty comfortable by my standards, and Cameron had managed without too much trouble too. However, there were eight of us planned for the first week, including visitors coming from Australia. Afterwards, the four of us would be living together for the next three months, so a few more home comforts would make life much easier and more pleasant.

One of the highest priorities, according to Moe, was a large oven. She is an accomplished home cook, and planned on working on her bread-making skills over the coming months. My cooking facilities for the previous months had been basic at best - I had a simple two burner propane stove which had initially sat on a plank of wood balanced on two makeshift sawhorses and then later, on a more stable kitchen counter top once I had it constructed.

I added an oven to the long list of items I needed to buy and jobs I needed to attend to. I looked in some of the Chinese supermarkets next time I was in town. In Bocas, as the town is on an island at the end of the delivery chain, things tend to be more expensive than elsewhere in Panama. Almirante, the port town on the mainland which is the departure point for water taxis to Bocas, tends to be a bit cheaper, but still doesn't offer much in the way of larger retail outlets. To really go shopping for bigger items you need to catch a local bus to David, one of Panama's bigger cities, about a four hour bus ride away. To make the trip worthwhile it is usually best to go one morning, stay overnight in David and return the next day. I wasn't particularly keen to go on a two day expedition just to buy an oven, so kept putting it off.

Another job I needed to attend to was making some curtain doors for my kitchen unit, which simply had open cupboard space under the counter. I had bought the material I wanted to use in town, and knew that my next door neighbour Janis had a sewing machine. She had become very interested in quilting, and had been learning under the expert guidance of another Dolphin Bay resident, Mary.

On Sunday, at Rana Azul, I had a chat with Mary, asking if she might be able to teach me enough about sewing to enable me to make my own set of curtain-doors for both my kitchen and bathroom. She said she would be happy to try, but it really depended upon how I fared as a student.

Paradise Delayed

A couple of days later I gathered my material and measurements. I collected Janis's sewing machine on the way past her house, heading across the bay to Carl and Mary's house, which sits high upon the hillside with a beautiful view over the whole of Dolphin Bay. She was a patient teacher, taking her time to shoed me the basics of measuring and cutting the material, setting up the sewing machine, and fabricating the curtains. I was very slow at first, but by lunchtime I had grasped some of the basics. After a lunch sat gazing over the bay and chatting with my hosts, I returned to my labours. By mid afternoon I was confident enough to return home to complete my work in my own time.

As Carl and Mary showed me out we passed Carl's little workshop. They showed me where they were building an extra room under the house, where a worker could stay overnight if the weather was too bad for him to return home.

"We need to find a small two ring cooker though, as we only have this oven which is far too big," Mary explained, pointing to a large item under a blue tarp.

"Where did the big oven come from and what are you planning to do with that?" I asked. Apparently they had just bought a new oven, and they really needed to sell the older one to make some more space.

"Do you know anyone looking for a big oven?" asked Mary.

Negotiations were quick and simple, and we came to a happy agreement. I just needed to get the oven home now.

"Maybe I could collect it next Sunday, either on the way down to Rana Azul, or on the way back?" It's always good to try to combine tasks, especially in my bigger boat, which isn't particularly cheap to run. Both the oven and someone else to help carry it wouldn't fit in *Ay Caramba*, at least not without serious risk of another sinking. Collecting the oven on Sunday would only involve a small detour that morning.

When I had returned from Canada Cameron and I had set off early on his last Sunday trip to Rana Azul, as I was keen to catch up with Bill and Janis first. On the way to their house I had been amazed to see a new place under construction, right by the little narrow cut through the peninsula of mangroves. It looked like I was getting new neighbours. The house had gone up quickly, Cameron told me, but nobody had any idea who was moving in.

A few days later I spotted a boat at the makeshift dock at the new property, and went to greet the newcomers. Brothers Kyle and Kent were building the house, with help from dad Skip and a local guy called

Oven relocation

Ricardo. Eventually Kent had moved in and I met his wife Marcie, who had arrived when construction reached the point where the house was habitable.

Now, with Bill and Janis away in the States for a while, I had been boat-sharing on a Sunday with Kent and Marcie, who were fun to hang out with.

They didn't always go out to Rana Azul, being keen to press on with work at the newly constructed house, so I stopped off at their house on the way home from Carl and Mary's to ask if they were planning to go that weekend. Yes, they would be happy to hitch a ride with me, and Kent was more than willing to assist with the oven moving.

"You'll be helping me out with something pretty soon, I imagine," he pointed out.

We decided to call at Carl and Mary's house in the morning, on the way down to Rana Azul. We figured it would probably be easier to manhandle the large oven down the steep path to the water while we were completely sober and there was plenty of daylight. There were no guarantees that either of these criteria would be in our favour as we headed home. After a cup of coffee and a tour of the beautiful property for Kent and Marcie, who were there for the first time, Kent and I lifted the oven between us. Pleasantly surprised at how light it was, we carefully made our way down the grassy path. I had a large tarp in the boat which we tied over the oven, as it would now be sitting out under the hot sun for the rest of the afternoon at the pizza restaurant. We said our thanks to our morning hosts, heading off across the bay again.

The afternoon was as much fun as always, but despite our best intentions, as is often the case, my boat was one of the last pulling away from the dock as the sun faded in the west. Time was against us, but if all went well there should be just enough daylight left to finish the relocation of the oven, I thought. We said our goodbyes to Steve and Jeanne, to whom I have said many hasty goodbyes as we hurriedly pull away from the restaurant dock in a last minute dash to get home before dark.

The trip home went well and we pulled into my bay in the half light, unloading the oven onto the dock quickly. The last leg of the journey involved carrying the oven about fifty yards to the house, and I looked into the boat trying to find my flip-flops. My heart sank as I realised that I had left them at the restaurant. I could picture exactly where they were, left at the entrance about six hours previously. Bare feet alone on the stony path would be painful enough, but carrying the oven, although not too heavy, would make the walk excruciating.

Paradise Delayed

"Er..." I began. "I'll just have to go up to the house to get some more flip flops. I left mine at Rana Azul." Marcie gave me a look to rival that which I received from Eric when I told him where the fuel was on the treacherous boat journey laden with logs. She looked pointedly out at the darkening sky and then back at me.

"I'll be quick," I promised, dashing off down the dock before Marcie could make any verbal comment.

The path underfoot was painful, but I tried to progress as quickly as possible. I considered taking to the grass, but it was filled with other potential hazards. Many very spiky plants grew in there, ants were common, and I had seen a scorpion or two as we had cleared the island the previous year. We had also seen a couple of snakes which my workers had assured me weren't poisonous, but with Panama boasting an impressive list of deadly serpents, I wasn't keen to take the risk.

The journey seemed to take forever as I tiptoed along the pathway. The trek was made more surreal by the solar lights which cast a very pale glow in the darkening evening. I'd had quite a few beers that afternoon which, I imagine, assisted in heightening the feeling of unreality. The walk, which would normally take about a minute, seemed to telescope into a marathon hike.

At the house I found another pair of flip-flops and headed back to the dock. The return journey was quicker, aided by adequate footwear, but still had an *Alice-In-Wonderland*-like quality to it, and again seemed to take an inordinate amount of time.

I apologised profusely for taking so long when I got back. Kent and I hefted the oven between us, him at the front and me behind. As we walked towards the house again in the growing darkness the situation struck me as ridiculous, and I started to laugh.

"What?" asked Kent over his shoulder.

"Do you ever take a look at what you are doing, and just ask yourself what on earth you are playing at? I mean look at us, fiddling about for hours with an oven, now stumbling across a darkened Caribbean island, just so Moe can bake bread when she gets here! Is this how you imagined this part of your life would be? Do you know what I mean?"

"I do!" Kent laughed. "If I was back at home in the States I'd just order an oven at the store, or maybe even online, and someone would deliver it to my house and install it for me."

"Exactly! But here it's half a day's effort just to get an oven to your house. And we've still got to get you home yet."

Oven relocation

Fortunately, there was enough of a moon up in a clear sky to find our way back to Kent and Marcie's house, where I dropped them at their dock, thanking them profusely. I found my way home without further trouble, and threw a cover over the oven on the balcony for the night. I had some kitchen re-modelling work to do the next day.

The oven looked great when I finally slid it back into the newly created gap in the kitchen counter. I was very much looking forward to the bread that it would produce in the near future.

Maxie's medicine

I met my friend Marty when I first moved to Australia in 2002. He was one of the four other occupants in the big shared house that I moved into, near to the beach.

We have stayed in touch over the years. I was very excited when Marty and his partner Carol said that they wanted to come and visit my little Panamanian island, along with their two kids, Bella, aged 12 and Maxie, a delightful 4 year old.

Moe and the kids arranged to fly into Panama City at the same time, and I flew from the little airport in Bocas to meet them all. We had a great couple of days in the city, and caught the overnight bus back to Bocas.

A couple of nights in a lovely beachfront resort were next on the list, courtesy of a friend who was looking after the place while it was closed for a short while. The weather was kind to us at the beachfront resort, but when we returned to the island, the rain set in for the next few days.

We had plenty to entertain us though, and made the best of our time as the weather worsened, and the winds picked up. The kids would play endlessly with the dog, and some of the friendlier chickens got more than their usual share of attention.

Maxie happily ran around barefoot most of the time, and at some point must have stood on something sharp which had cut her foot. I don't think she'd even noticed when it had happened. Towards the end of the week, however, Marty and Carol had become more worried about the foot as there seemed to be some infection.

A call was made over the VHF radio, and a long discussion with one of the gringo ex-pat doctors living nearby convinced Marty and Carol that the need for antibiotics was imperative.

It was by now about 4pm on a stormy Saturday afternoon, and the pharmacy in town, probably half an hour away by boat in this weather, would probably close at 5pm. If we were going to go it had to be right now.

I collected the petrol can and headed to the dock to begin preparing the bigger boat for the trip to town. I started the engine to begin warming it up, waiting while the others decided who was going and who was staying.

Maxie's medicine

I looked beyond my little protected bay, which was being whipped by the wind pushing directly into it. I could see whitecaps on the waves and dark skies above. It was going to be a rough journey.

With my phone securely sealed in two plastic bags, I promised Moe that I would call when we got to town. Marty and Carol had decided to bring Maxie along, hoping that the pharmacist would be able to offer further advice.

The four of us donned our lifejackets, mine with an engine cut-off switch attached to it which would kill the engine should I foolishly fall overboard - I had no plans to do so.

We set out of the bay and at first it seemed like the journey would be relatively straightforward, but as soon as we reached deeper water the size and force of the waves became apparent.

The boat handled the heavy swell well, and we were lucky to be heading straight into the waves, which meant we mainly just rode up and over them. At times though the bow of the boat would catch in the following wave and throw a huge spray of water into the boat.

Occasionally, as I tried to keep the speed of the boat up to keep it planing along, we would launch off the top of a tall wave and drop into the trough behind it with a sickening lurch.

About halfway to town the waves were at their highest. I had to back the throttle down to an idle and simply keep the boat heading forward into the mounting waves.

Maxie had simply buried her head in her mum's lap, obviously not wanting to experience any of the stormy trip. I imagine she was just wishing she was somewhere else. I was wishing much the same thing.

Eventually we neared town. In the lee of the main island the waves subsided, and we made better progress, arriving at the dock just after 5pm. A mad dash got us to the pharmacy just before they locked the doors, and antibiotics were duly purchased.

I was now more concerned about the return journey. On the trip northwards into town we were coming into the waves, which although slow, is relatively easy. On the way home the huge waves would be behind us, pushing us forward. If we were caught and picked up by one of the larger ones we would end up surfing the boat down the face of the wave with very little control. I had experienced this to a small degree in much lighter seas, and knew how easy it would be in these conditions to lose control of the boat and tip it over.

Paradise Delayed

I voiced my concerns to Marty, who suggested that if we needed to, maybe we should stay in a hotel in town for the night. It was an option I had considered too.

We made a few quick shopping purchases and headed back to the dock. It was difficult to tell from the safety of shore what it was like out in the bay, but the skies had cleared a bit and we still had time to get home before dark. I decided that we should give it a go and see what conditions were like. We would turn around and come back to town if it was too bad.

The change in conditions was amazing. The storm seemed to have blown itself out and the sea had calmed down quite a bit. We made a run diagonally across the waves, heading for cover in the lee of Isla Cristobal, as the wind seemed to have shifted a little too.

Maxie decided that the best spot for her was down on the bottom of the boat. She stayed there for the whole journey, kneeling on the floor, holding onto one of the cross spars, her head on her hands. Carol could not coax her back on to her lap at all.

The journey was still pretty wild, but the boat handled well, and there no longer seemed to be any danger of losing control on a larger wave. We made good time on the return journey, only getting swamped by one large wave which crashed across the bows. As the water rolled down the floor of the boat Maxie disappeared under it for a second, but quickly reappeared, still clutching the cross spar tightly.

We made it back to the island just before dark, to the surprise of Moe and her kids at home. The last they had heard from us was when we were seriously considering a night in a hotel. They had settled in to watch a movie and were a little disappointed when we had interrupted it.

Maxie was given some more antibiotics, and the next morning seemed to be none-the-worse for the whole experience.

"Are we going in the boat again today Ian?" she asked me brightly.

"I'd rather not," I answered, not telling her that the day before had been the worst crossing to town I had ever experienced. "But we have to get you guys to the airport."

The sea was still rough, but fortunately didn't rival the previous day's wild crossing. Maxie enjoyed the second journey much more. She was feeling much better, and of course was now a seasoned seafarer.

A Caribbean Christmas

With a great majority of the residents of the archipelago being either retired or semi-retired, social events and occasions are very much enjoyed. Parties and gatherings are often arranged throughout the week, with Sunday being saved for the big communal gathering day at Rana Azul.

As Christmas approached the invites started rolling in and Maible had to be appointed as social secretary. She made a calendar which went up on the fridge door, and kept us informed of when and where we would be going.

The biggest event by far was going to be Christmas Day at Cynde's house. Cynde is one of the mainstays of the Bocas social world. She has a wonderful house built on the water's edge, with a huge balcony, ideal for hosting large groups of people. The balcony overlooks some beautiful coral reef, and great big fat snapper fish swim lazily round the dock pilings.

I can't help but think how her fish would look under a grill, but Cynde will have none of it. She feeds them occasionally with a handful of dried dog food which the fish consume enthusiastically. I'm sure she thinks of them almost as pets.

Everyone was invited to Cynde's for Christmas Day. As on all social occasions, the food for the day would be a pot-luck. Cynde would cook the turkey; everyone else would bring a dish, perhaps vegetables, salad or a desert. And a cooler full of beer too, of course.

Early on Christmas morning we opened our family presents at home. The unwrapping ceremonies were followed by a light breakfast, in anticipation of a big meal in the afternoon.

Moe had been using the big oven at the house enthusiastically, and was becoming something of a bread baking expert. She had made all sorts of breads, both savoury and sweet. The kids and I would hover around the kitchen each day when the baking was done, keen to try the new results. She usually made some bread-based dish for many of the parties to which we went, often involving the local cacao to make some sort of chocolaty treat. After opening all of her presents, for Cynde's party, she made an antipasto platter, with crispy herbed toasts.

We collected Kent and Marcie on the way. At Cynde's house the party was already in full swing, and over the next hour or so more people arrived. I think there must have been around forty people there by the time dinner was served. The food was wonderful, with a huge and tasty tourtière (a delicious Canadian type of meat pie), sumptuous turkey, and a wealth of side dishes. The choice of desserts was extensive too, highlighted by a key lime pie, the pieces of which disappeared rather quickly.

The other highlight of the afternoon was the Yankee Swap Christmas gift exchange. Almost everyone had brought along a wrapped gift, our remit having been to spend around $10 on a mystery present. Numbers were drawn and the chaotic fun began. There was much stealing and swapping of presents as the game unfolded, and many of the gifts were very imaginative and amusing.

There was much laughter and by the end of the afternoon my cheeks ached from smiling so much. Our family came home with a small wooden tea tray, a bottle of champagne, a copy of a book written by a local ex-pat, and Finn was extremely pleased to end up owning the hotly contested switchblade knife.

On the way home I again thought about the wonderful community in which I had found myself, and the people here who made the lagoon such a special place to live.

Kent's boat

The noise had started quietly, unobtrusively at first, but I knew it meant trouble - a quiet *tick tick tick* from very low down at the back of the boat. Nobody else noticed at first. I had Moe drive the boat for a while so I could get close to the engine and listen. It certainly sounded like it was coming from low down, towards the bottom of the engine shaft, where the propeller and gearbox are located.

We had only had the new boat a couple of weeks and I couldn't believe it had already developed a problem. I had been offered an exchange. Our friend Rick needed a bigger workboat, and he wondered if I would be interested in swapping my big boat for his little blue James Bond-style speedboat. I didn't use the big boat much, no longer needing it for construction purposes, so I was tempted. We had made a provisional exchange, and all had gone well. A week later the exchange had become permanent.

Another week after that the ticking noise had started.

We made it home that day without trouble, and a few days later, on our next excursion in the boat, the problem hadn't somehow miraculously resolved itself. It hadn't got any worse though. I needed to check the gearbox oil as soon as possible.

As always, other matters took priority and checking the gearbox oil slipped down the list. December 21st rolled around, along with our invite to spend the afternoon on our friend's luxurious motor yacht at their "Solstice Party" - just another excuse to sit in the sun and enjoy a few beers with friends.

Second Star was moored in the southern anchorage, very close to town. We managed to combine an afternoon of shopping with an early evening of drinking with Johne and Aeon and their other guests, before setting off for home as the sun sank in the west. Hopefully we'd make it before dark.

As I throttled the boat up and turned to the south, the ticking noise from the gearbox, still unchecked, suddenly developed into what could now be described as a loud *clacking*. I slowed the boat, put it in neutral, and clambered over the groceries to take a look, muttering under my breath. Why hadn't I changed the gearbox oil before now?

Needless to say, there was no visible evidence - nothing as simple as something caught around the prop. I knew the trouble was inside and was potentially expensive.

Paradise Delayed

We nursed the boat home slowly in the gathering dark, just reaching our dock before night fell completely. I tied the boat up, not really wanting to consider the problems ahead. Christmas was only a few days away and, just like last year, my boat engine was failing me again.

I wanted a second opinion. The next morning I nursed the boat around to my neighbour's house. Kent and Marcie were progressing well with their house on a small piece of land just around the corner from my property, so were only a few minutes away by boat. Kent had a lot of experience with boats, so I would be grateful for his opinion on the noises issuing from mine.

"Yep, sounds like the gearbox to me," he said, confirming my own diagnosis. "Let's see how the oil looks." He whipped out some tools. By loosening the top screw of the gearbox oil sump we managed to release a small sample of oil.

"Oh dear," he said, rubbing the oil thoughtfully between his fingers. "Look at this. There is a lot of metal glistening in here. Something is getting ground to pieces in there. We're going to have to pull the gearbox apart to see what's going on."

Kent suggested that he could come round the next morning so we could pull the bottom off the engine to discover the cause of the problem. If I could get the parts ordered before the New Year, he suggested, we'd have the boat up and running by mid-January. From my previous experience with the big Yamaha 75, I knew this to be wildly optimistic at best, but Kent was willing to help for the price of a few beers, and I didn't want to discourage him.

Waist deep in water, stood on a plank of wood to stop our feet sinking into the mud on the seabed, Kent and I worked on the engine while Finn and Maible provided coffee and biscuits. Eventually we freed the gearbox from the motor and took it to the shed to examine it more closely. The oil looked like glitter paint, glimmering with thousands of tiny pieces of metal, obviously from the cogs inside the gearbox. Without one particular tool we needed, Kent was unable to open the gearbox right then, but by turning the drive shaft manually, it was extremely obvious that all was not well within. The shaft didn't turn smoothly as it should, but grated from one notch to the next when rotated in one direction, and was impossible to turn the other way at all.

I thanked Kent profusely for his time, and we retired to the house to clean up, open a couple of beers and start some internet research on prices and possibilities. With the engine being an older model Johnson which was no longer in production I thought I may run in to trouble sourcing parts.

Kent's boat

However, since it was such a common and popular engine I was pleased to discover I wasn't going to have any problems finding what I needed. Paying for the parts was obviously going to be the issue - for just the three main gear cogs I would probably need, the going price seemed to be around $500.

I was still going to have to strip the engine further to find out exactly what was needed, which would probably incur further cost too. Kent commiserated with me, apologised for not having the tools we needed to fully strip down the gearbox, offered to help again when I had what I needed, and very kindly offered to lend me his boat if I needed it before I could get mine fixed.

I hoped it wouldn't come to that, as I still had the little boat with the 25 horsepower engine on it. That was fine for transporting the four of us around, but couldn't carry much more when we were all in it. I thanked him again for his time and kindness, but said that I thought we would manage.

"It's no trouble at all. Please don't hesitate to ask if you need to use it." He was obviously quite sincere and once again I marvelled at the wonderful nature of the type of people that came to Bocas to build a new life.

Christmas came and went, parties were enjoyed by all, and our little boat served us proudly, running us quickly and efficiently around Dolphin Bay from one social engagement to the next. But with supplies running low and more social events pencilled in on the calendar around the New Year, a trip to town was obviously going to be needed. Moe had a big list of requirements for baking ingredients, as all social occasions in the bay are run on a pot-luck basis, with each attendee bringing a plate and their own drinks to the event.

Maybe we could borrow Kent's boat just once to make one big shopping trip? We really didn't like the idea, reluctant to ask for further favours and reluctant to borrow someone else's boat. With boats being such an integral part of day-to-day life, if anything happened to Kent's boat while in my possession... well, it just didn't bear thinking about.

But by now I was pretty confident about my boat handling skills. We would only be going to town and back, a route I knew well and which held no danger of uncharted reef damage to the boat or engine. We'd only need the boat for the afternoon. What could possibly go wrong?

I spoke to Kent, who said he was happy to let us use it, as he had no need for the boat the next day. Marcie asked if we could grab a few small items in town for her and gave us a list. Bringing back a few grocery items for them would in no way repaid the kindness they had shown us in the past few days though.

"Ah, don't worry about it," Kent told me happily. "What goes around comes around. The boot will be on the other foot soon enough, I imagine," he laughed. "That's how it is with boats."

The next morning I took our little boat around the corner to Kent's house, hefted the fuel tank out of it into Kent's boat and offered more profuse thanks. I headed back home to collect Moe and the kids.

There was quite a degree of excitement about the day, as Kent's boat was a significant step up the marine ladder from mine. Although my new boat, now in pieces, had console steering, as opposed to tiller steering at the rear, it didn't have a huge 140 horsepower engine on the back. Kent's boat was fast and smooth, and for once I didn't worry about fuel consumption, simply enjoying driving the powerful boat towards town.

There was also great excitement about the day as we had an invite that evening to dine aboard our friends' yacht, *Second Star*. Johne and Aeon were going to pull up anchor in the south anchorage shortly after lunch, planning to head down to Dolphin Bay in the afternoon. The kids had been offered the opportunity to take the helm of the yacht on the journey south. The easiest way to return from town was to tow Kent's boat behind the big yacht.

We were as efficient as usual on our shopping trip, managing to get some laundry done, change one of our propane bottles and re-stock our beer supply.

At the beautiful *Second Star* preparations for departure were underway as we arrived. Before long we had their little boat hoisted up onto the top deck, with Kent's boat hitched up behind. Maible and Finn both took a turn at driving the motor yacht while Moe chatted with Aeon, who kept a watchful eye on things at the helm. Johne and I sat out on the foredeck sipping icy-cold beers.

At Dolphin Bay we dropped anchor and jumped back into Kent's boat to take our groceries home. We unloaded our large haul of produce and packed it all away, taking turns in the shower to prepare to go out for the evening, back to *Second Star* for dinner.

The weather was deteriorating, and by early evening, as the sky darkened, a steady rain had started falling. We all packed a plastic bag of dry clothes, a fairly common requirement in Dolphin Bay. Back in Kent's boat we drove around the corner to drop it off. Moe dropped off Marcie's groceries, along with some fat cigars I had bought Kent as a

Kent's boat

little thank-you gift. I put the fuel can back in our boat, connected the fuel line, pumped the bulb to prime the engine and pulled the starter cord. It usually took a few pulls to get the boat started, but I had the technique down pat by now. The engine fired into life despite the downpour, and Moe and the kids climbed in carefully.

We waved our goodbyes as I put the engine into reverse. There was the usual click as reverse engaged and we pulled back from the dock. I shifted into neutral, but something didn't feel quite right as I pulled the gear selector further forward. I revved the engine, but nothing happened. I shifted the lever again, but it felt very loose. I couldn't engage either forward or reverse now, and the boat slowly drifted further from the dock as the rain pounded down.

Fortunately we had a paddle with us and Finn soon paddled us back to Kent's dock where Moe and the kids climbed out again. Kent returned to the dock and climbed into the boat with me, the pair of us being careful not to shift too much weight to the back, wary of sinking the small boat. I took the engine hood off and we peered into the innards of the engine. It was difficult to see anything in the gathering darkness with rainwater dripping off our noses, and Kent was quick to make an offer.

"Just take my boat for now. Leave this one here and come back in the morning when the weather clears. We'll take a look at it then." He was obviously keen to return to the TV show they had been watching on their computer when we had arrived.

I thanked him profusely once more, swapping the fuel can back again. We were finally on our way to dinner. The rainy weather hadn't let up by 10pm when we decided to head for home, and we made our way slowly through the mangroves in very dark conditions.

At our dock I made sure the boat was tied securely before we headed for bed.

It rained heavily during the night, but not enough to cause me any concerns. On rare occasions I used to have had to get up in a torrential downpour to go and bail out the smaller of my two boats. I always keep the bigger boat under the roof of the dock, but there isn't room under there for the smaller one too.

My previous experience of discovering *Ay Caramba* on the seabed one morning after a very stormy night, the engine fortunately still just out of the water, had caused me to make some changes in my docking systems.

"You're not really a local," I had been told by a few people, "until you've sunk your first boat." The little boat hadn't taken much effort to

Paradise Delayed

re-float. All I'd had to do was jump in beside it, lift the back close to the surface and start bailing. I soon emptied the boat and had it floating again, the engine and hull none the worse for the sinking. I'd been very lucky, and after that morning I certainly felt like a true local.

Since then I had moved *Ay Caramba*'s docking location to slightly shallower water. With two tyres placed on the sea floor under the rear of the boat, the propeller of the engine slotted neatly between the tyres, there was no real danger anymore If the boat filled overnight it would only drop a few inches and the back of it would sit on the tyres, keeping the engine well above water.

I now slept peacefully at night, not worried about how hard the rain might fall. However, with Kent's boat at the dock for the night and the rain pounding down, my peaceful sleep was unjustified.

In the morning Moe and Maible went for a walk around the island, but Maible returned very quickly.

"There's a bit of a problem with Kent's boat," she reported, wide-eyed.

At worst there could be a few inches of water in it, I thought, as it was a big boat, and I hadn't been aware of that much rain. I followed Maible back to the dock, where I stared in horror at what I saw.

I had parked Kent's boat alongside the dock with its nose pointing towards the shore where *Ay Caramba* usually sat, the engine out in slightly deeper water. Somehow the hull had filled completely with water, and was now sat on the seabed, the engine cowling touching the water, but not quite underneath. I may have simply stood there frozen with shock for a second or two.

I remember putting my hands on my head in despair, saying, "That's it. I'm completely screwed now!" My choice of language may have actually been a bit more colourful than that.

Kent's engine was something that was way beyond what my remaining funds could cover. If seawater had entered it at all, it would be ruined.

Once the initial shock had worn off we started trying to figure out what to do next. "We have to get that emptied out and floating again," I said. "How on earth are we going to do that?"

The kids were sent back to the house for shoes for everyone, as well as a set of buckets and other bailing items. When they got back Moe and I got in the water, still trying to figure out what to do. Bailing obviously wasn't going to achieve anything, as the transom of the boat was underwater, held down by the weight of the engine. Bailed buckets from

Kent's boat

inside the boat would just be replaced by water flowing in over the transom. We needed to get the transom above the water level, so we could bail water out without it flowing back in at the same rate.

Moe and I tried lifting the back of the boat a little, but the weight forced our feet deep into the mud of the sea floor. Seeing the gravity of the situation, Finn jumped in the water to help out. Once our feet hit more supportive material we were able to start lifting together, although we were now almost chest-deep in the water. Lifting very slowly and co-ordinating our efforts we could raise the boat a little. Allowing time for the water to flow out over the transom, we eventually got the engine completely above water.

We managed to get the transom level with the surface and had Maible tie the stern ropes as tight as possible. When we released the boat to try to bail, the weight of the engine stretched the ropes taught, the back of the boat sank a couple of inches, and the cleats screwed into the wood of the dock groaned under the strain. The transom was back underwater, and bailing would have been pointless anyway. Moe and I quickly lifted the back of the boat again, worried that we might wreck the dock, or snap one of the lines.

I was very concerned that as the boat sank again it may settle a little deeper than last time, as we had disturbed the sediment on the seabed. We didn't have an inch to spare. If the engine dropped any further damage would be inevitable.

Very carefully we took turns at supporting the boat while the other retrieved their shoes from the deep mud, and we re-assessed our options. Moe suggested we leverage the boat forward, into shallower waters. Plan B involved having Finn move the two kayukos, our local-style canoes. They were bobbing happily in the shallows in front of Kent's boat, half full of water, but still floating, being made of light wood. With clear space ahead of us Moe, Finn and I lifted together again. Maible pulled the bow rope from the dock as we pushed the boat forward towards shallower water.

With a couple of good efforts we managed to shift the waterlogged craft forwards by more than a full boat length, into much shallower water. With an extra final effort we managed to position the front of the hull between the two tyres on which the back of *Ay Caramba* usually sat. The back of the boat was now much higher as it sat on the seabed once again, the engine well clear of the water, but the transom still under, almost level with the surface.

Paradise Delayed

Moe and I lifted again, raising the transom once more while Finn and Maible bailed, Finn still in the water with us, Maible laid on the dock reaching down with her smaller bucket. For a moment I thought we were making progress, but the bailing actions within the boat caused the water to slosh back and forth inside the hull, meaning Moe and I couldn't keep the boat balanced properly. The transom would keep dipping under, allowing water to rush back in. We were almost back where we had started.

We paused for a rest and had another re-think. Inspired by the front of the hull now sitting on the tyres in the shallow water by the shore, I suggested we gather another couple of tyres for the back of the boat. Maible grabbed one of the spare ones that had been sitting on the dock, waiting for the day I would get around to tying them to the posts to act as extra boat buffers. She rolled it along the dock to us.

We dropped it in by the back of the boat, and as Moe lifted again, I carefully positioned the tyre under the rear right corner. We repeated the process, deciding to lift the right side higher to add a second tyre. We could then combine our efforts, lifting the left of the boat and levering it up onto the tyres under the other side.

It worked a treat. We managed to get the transom just above the water line. It was much more stable this time, and the sloshing around while the kids bailed didn't rock the boat so much.

They bailed and bailed, and ever so slowly the water level began to drop inside the boat. Moe and I strained to keep the boat steady. If we let it drop at all we would lose all the precious ground we had made - the transom was only an inch or so above the waterline.

We changed positions carefully, Moe bailing for a while as Finn and I supported the boat, then again to allow me to take a turn with the bailer. With every precious inch we gained, as the water level in the boat dropped, the task of supporting it became slightly easier. Eventually we felt confident enough to allow the boat to float unsupported, still three-quarters swamped. We could all bail then, and progress speeded up. Eventually I felt confident enough to allow Maible to climb into the boat and bail from within.

We had clearly won the battle now, the danger of the boat slipping under again gone. It was only a matter of time before all the water was removed from the hull, and we could take a look at the damage.

I took the cover off the top of the engine and looked inside fearfully, but all looked very dry. Moe and the kids wiped and cleaned the inside of the boat, and I looked under the rear of the boat where the battery was stored.

Kent's boat

The terminals were incredibly corroded, one having rotted off completely. I guessed the battery had shorted out when the water had risen over the top of it, making a direct connection between positive and negative terminal.

How on earth had so much water got into the boat, we wondered? I couldn't figure it out, unless the vinyl roof of the boat had just gathered so much water, and instead of shedding it overboard, had drained it into the boat. Maybe there had been a wind that had made some bigger waves that had swamped the boat from the back - but we hadn't heard any wind during the night, and the waters were pretty calm this morning, just a light breeze blowing into the bay from the north. Mysterious.

I knew that next I had to go round to Kent and Marcie's house and face the music. I didn't relish the thought of telling Kent what had happened. They had been incredibly kind and trusting to lend us the boat. In less than 24 hours I had betrayed that trust in a big way, without even know how the incident had occurred.

I didn't want to try starting the boat, as I wanted Kent to take a look at it first to satisfy himself that there was no water in the engine. So with my bigger boat out of action, and the smaller one left at Kent's house the night before, I had no choice but to paddle round to see them in one of the kayukos.

I pulled up at their dock and walked up to the house, shouting a subdued "Hello." In the house I began my sorry tale with, "I'm afraid there's good news and there's bad news... I'll start with the good." I told them what had happened, emphasising the fact that I didn't think that the engine would have any water in it. However, I went on, the bad news was that the battery was certainly ruined and there was the concern about the electric cables and steering apparatus. I apologised profusely, and waited for the response.

Kent was breezily dismissive of the disaster. "That's boating, isn't it? It's not the first one I've had sunk and it probably won't be the last. Come on, we'll go and take a look. I'll gather some tools."

I couldn't believe how well they both took it. I repeated my abject apologies, but Kent would have no more of it, keen to go and take a look at the engine. What wonderful neighbours, I thought - I had expected a possible punch on the nose, and would probably have deserved it.

Kent fiddled with the gear shifter on my little boat, which had come loose under the engine cowling the previous night. "I think we can manually put it into forward gear," he told me, "just to get us around to your house."

Paradise Delayed

We loaded his tools into the little boat and jumped in. I headed to the back of the boat, where I spotted that we needed one more item, and my heart sank a little.

"Ahhh, fuel?" I said, half statement and half question. In my hurry to get around to Kent's house and get the inevitable confession over and done with I hadn't thought to bring a can of fuel. It's not really the first thing you think of when you get into a kayuko. "Do you have any here Kent?" I asked hopefully.

He gave me a look that was very similar to the one Eric had given me about a year earlier, when we realised that the fuel cans were in the locker which was buried under the huge pile of logs in the boat - utter disbelief.

"My fuel cans were in my boat," he said. At least they had been safely locked in my shed overnight, and weren't floating around the bay this morning.

"And you don't have a spare here?"

"Unfortunately not. No."

"Right, looks like we're paddling then," I said brightly, hoping to create an optimistic feeling of cheery enthusiasm for a bracing morning of exercise. Kent didn't seem quite so enthusiastic, but agreed that it was the only answer, unless I cared to paddle the kayuko back alone and return with some fuel. We discussed using the kayuko, which performs well with Moe and one of the kids paddling together, but we rejected the idea, as two grown men would be much more unstable, and Kent had no desire to loose his tools to the sea.

So our decision was to paddle little *Ay Caramba* around to my house. We were lucky that there was one paddle in the little boat to go with the one I had used to paddle the kayuko. We started by standing up, as the paddles are pretty long, Kent at the front and me behind, one paddling on either side. Our first problem was the engine, which would swing slowly from side to side as we moved about, acting like a rudder, counteracting our paddling efforts.

With the engine being fairly old, it would no longer pivot up out of the water, the pivot mechanism being somewhat rusty. I had to keep nudging the tiller with my foot to keep the boat on a roughly straight course. Too much nudging and we would veer off in one direction, not enough nudging and the engine would slowly pivot the other way, causing an inexorable change of direction for which our paddling efforts eventually could not compensate.

I finally got the rhythm right - paddle, paddle, paddle, nudge, paddle paddle paddle, nudge - and we headed out of Kent's little bay in front of his house. By now the wind had picked up a little and we were heading northwards through the wide mangrove cut, straight into the breeze This slowed our progress considerably. I had to adjust my paddle to nudge ratio to compensate for the wind, depending on whether it was trying to push the front of the little boat to the left or the right. It was incredibly frustrating and I made more apologies. We tried to hug the mangroves closely, where there was a little shelter from the wind. We also tried sitting down to reduce our wind resistance. When sitting it was much easier to control the engine and keep us on course, as I could just hold it in place with my knee, but it was much harder work paddling with the long paddles in that position.

At one point a boat sped by, filled to the brim with tourists out to view the dolphins in Dolphin Bay. Several waved, raising their cameras to record the sight of the two gringos paddling a boat with an engine on the back. The tour operator obviously didn't see any need to stop to offer help.

We swapped from side to side, front to back, stood up and sat down, then back through the various options again to give our aching arms and shoulders a rest. We finally made it to the end of the section of the wide channel through the mangroves which ran in a north-south direction, finally turning to the east, now in the lee of the mangroves to our left. We started to make better progress.

"Remember when you helped me collect my oven?" I asked Kent, as we took a well-earned breather. To my relief he burst out laughing, obviously able to see the funny side of the current ridiculous situation. "Well, here's another one of those Caribbean moments. Just look at what we are doing. This is absolutely ridiculous. I really must apologise again." I was laughing too now.

"Yes, living the dream, aren't we?" he spluttered, and we both laughed helplessly.

Back at my dock the other three had been busy. They had cleaned and polished Kent's boat, drying everything inside as well as possible. It looked immaculate. We removed the top from Kent's engine once more, peering inside together. "Looks pretty dry," said Kent, "but let's pull the air filter off just to be sure. The carburettors were at the front end of the engine which had been closest to the water. They were therefore the most likely to have had water enter them.

Paradise Delayed

Kent opened the screws at the bottom of the float bowls and drained the fuel out, which didn't show any sign of water in it, then re-assembled everything. We attached a fuel can recovered from my shed and took the battery from my out-of-commission larger boat. After a brief search through my container of nuts and bolts for two new connections for the battery terminals we were ready for testing.

Kent gave the fuel bulb a couple of pumps to refill the carbs. My heart was in my mouth as he turned the key. Nothing. He explained that the solenoid which turned on his starter motor hadn't been working for some time, which was why there was no response. He found the starter tool he had fashioned from a length of battery cable. Bridging from the gap from the battery cable to the starter motor caused the engine to crank. It coughed fitfully then fired into glorious life. We looked at each other and nodded in quiet satisfaction.

We put the tools away, and up at the house we cleaned ourselves up. I produced a couple of cold beers from the fridge.

"Just the little boat to fix now," said Kent, raising his bottle, "and then the gearbox on the other one. And my starter motor."

"Yes," I said, raising my bottle. "Here's to living the dream."

"Living the dream." He laughed as we clinked bottles.

I'm pretty sure that was the moment Kent stopped being my neighbour and became a good friend.

Secret lagoon

"What does everyone want to do today?" I had asked the family. "It's a beautiful sunny morning and I think we should get out there and enjoy it." It was Saturday so Moe didn't have to home-school the kids in the morning. The day was ours.

In response to the general chorus of "I don't know"s and half-hearted ideas about snorkelling, I said, "I have a suggestion then. Who wants to go and explore a secret lagoon?" The verdict was unanimous.

We loaded the small boat, whose gear shifter had recently been fixed by Kent with relative ease, and set off for a large area of mangroves a couple of miles away. I had been studying aerial photography of the area on Google Earth, and had found what looked like a large body of open water completely enclosed and hidden inside a mangrove island. There were no houses anywhere nearby, and in over a year of living here, I had never heard anybody mention this place. Surely it was worth investigating?

The journey took us about ten minutes, and we approached the mangroves cautiously, wary of any shallow reef. I knew roughly where to look, and we all peered through the mangroves.

"Yes, I can see open water through there," exclaimed Moe. We tied the boat to a large mangrove root.

With closed shoes brought along for the purpose, Moe and I scrambled through the mangroves, over the roots and under the branches, wary of sharp barnacles below and spider webs higher up. The kids stayed in the boat, letting us break the new trail, more interested in the multitude of tropical fish under the boat than getting spiders in their hair.

We only had to go twenty yards or so. We came out on the edge of a lake about a hundred yards across and almost perfectly circular. From what we could see there was no entrance or exit. The place was completely hidden from view from the outside. It truly was a secret lagoon. The water seemed to be pretty deep even at the edge where we stood, and the corals growing on the roots of the mangroves were amazing, their growth obviously undisturbed by boats or people.

We had brought a mask with us. Moe shouted for Finn to bring it over. How deep was the water? Maybe there were some big fish in here, like the corals, left to grow undisturbed?

I could see that the water was deep enough to jump in, and did so with slight trepidation. Were there big fish? How would I get out again, as the

Paradise Delayed

mangrove roots were so overgrown with huge corals? In the water the colours were amazing, but the bottom dropped off sharply just a few feet beyond the mangroves, quickly disappearing into the gloom below. I had a quick swim around, then found some reasonable clear roots and with Moe's help hauled myself up onto the mangroves again.

"We should come back with a kayuko," I suggested, "and drag it over the mangrove roots into the lagoon. I bet there is some amazing stuff in here."

We kept our find a secret the next day at Rana Azul. On Monday afternoon, after school, a second expedition was mounted, this time with our bigger kayuko in tow.

The little boat had seemed to be using more fuel recently. On the trip on Saturday to the lagoon I had been surprised that the fuel tank seemed much lighter than I expected when I lifted it out of the boat at the end of the journey. On the journey to Rana Azul the usually economical engine wolfed almost half a tank, which was alarming. I had discussed the problem with Kent.

"Could be the fuel pump or a fuel leak somewhere, but I'm afraid it's more likely to be the piston rings," he told me.

We'd made it home on Sunday and I'd refilled the tank for our Monday expedition, confident that even towing the kayuko behind us, we'd be fine for such a short journey.

At the mangrove island we tied up at our previous spot, and between us hoisted the kayuko past the little boat and up onto the roots of the mangroves. Pushing and pulling, we picked an easy route. The wooden canoe slipped easily across the roots and splashed down into the lagoon. I planned to snorkel across, this time fully equipped with mask, snorkel and fins, along with a pair of gloves too. The other three would paddle the kayuko around together, following my progress.

In the water I took a direct line across the lagoon and was soon over deep water. I dived down in the centre, guessing the depth to be about twenty to twenty five feet. The bottom was sandy and devoid of much life. The water was home to a host of jellyfish. At the far side there were more amazing corals around the mangrove roots, but to my disappointment, not many bigger fish.

We followed the edge around to the right, back to our start point, then took a direct route across once more and followed the edge around in the other direction. Mischievous as always, I decided to give occupants of the kayuko a little surprise. I quietly picked a large moon jelly up in my

Secret lagoon

hand and swam close to the kayuko. I casually tossed it in, right into Finn's lap. He screamed in terror and jumped up, nearly capsizing the overloaded kayuko. Between bouts of laughter, Moe pointed out to him that if he tipped the boat, he would be swimming in a whole pool of jellyfish. The jellyfish was released and balance was restored.

About twenty yards before we reached our start point again we were surprised to find a small cut through the mangroves, just wide enough for the kayuko, leading back to the open water outside. We were a little disappointed. We obviously weren't the only ones that came here. However, the cut saved us from having to pull the kayuko back through the mangroves when we were ready to leave.

Finn was keen to paddle the kayuko home on his own, craving some tough exercise. He felt he didn't get enough exercise on the island, so he set off before us, paddling confidently. The three of us explored the crystal clear water of the bay outside the lagoon for a while, which was mercifully free of jellyfish. Diving to the bottom to examine a big head of coral, I was surprised to find a small nurse shark hiding underneath. It was perhaps four feet long, and paid no notice to me at all, even when I stroked its tail nervously.

We eventually set off for home, looking for Finn on the way, keen to see how he was faring on his own on open water. As we rounded the corner of the little sheltered bay we discovered that the wind had picked up. The sea was much rougher than when we had come out earlier on. The waves were picking up, and Moe was worried about Finn. She needn't have worried though, as when we caught up with him he had a huge grin on his face, obviously thoroughly enjoying the challenge. We suggested he take the same route we planned, going into Dolphin Bay where it would be much more sheltered, rather than taking the shorter but much more exposed direct route home.

Inside the entrance of the bay we waited to make sure he knew the way, and giving him a last wave, we set off for home. We hadn't gone too far when the engine coughed and spluttered, then died. It had been doing this occasionally recently, and I pumped the fuel bulb and fired it up again. Less than a minute later the engine died again. Confused, I tested the weight of the fuel tank, alarmed to feel it almost empty. How could we have used so much fuel on such a short journey?

We had just passed a local couple in a kayuko, and they now paddled calmly by as I fiddled with the fuel tank, giving us another friendly wave. With the engine running again we passed them a second time, waving once more, only to have the engine die again ten yards further on. They paddled past with confused looks on their faces. For a few minutes we

Paradise Delayed

kept leapfrogging each other, as our engine ran in brief bursts. They must have wondered what these strange gringos were up to.

I tipped the tank so the last dregs of fuel pooled in the corner by the fuel pipe outlet, and we managed another minute before the engine coughed its last. We weren't too far from home now. I had been aiming for Kent and Marcie's house, which we would pass on the way. The engine had died about a quarter of a mile from our goal and we were now in a bit of trouble. We only had one paddle with us, as Finn was using the other, and the boat had stopped in a tricky location. We were just to the south of the wide passage which ran up through the mangroves to our house, so were exposed to the wind once again, which was blowing from the north. We were about fifty yards from the mangroves. As the boat coasted to a stop I could see the danger.

"If we don't get to those mangroves quickly the wind will catch us, and the next stop will be right down at the south end of the bay, maybe at Carl and Mary's if we get lucky." I started paddling as hard as I could. Moe and Maible paddled with their hands, but we were only making very slow progress. We tried for a while, but I could see we would all tire before we reached the shelter of the mangroves.

Maible piped up with a bright suggestion. "Why don't we swim behind the boat and push it?"

"Here! Paddle with this," I told Moe, handing her the paddle. I grabbed my fins and jumped overboard. Maible followed suit and in the water behind the boat we finned as hard as we could, grinning at each other at the ridiculous situation we found ourselves in.

We made better progress like this. Working as a team, turning the engine to act like a rudder as Kent and I had done before, we finally made it to the shelter of the mangroves, out of the windy danger zone. It was now simply a matter of plodding on as we were and we'd eventually reach our destination. That quarter of a mile seemed like such a long way that day but, tired to the point of exhaustion, we finally arrived as the first hint of dusk was darkening the sky.

Moe was very worried about Finn. She tried calling him on the mobile phone we had given him as a safety net for his voyage, while I went to find Kent. Unfortunately Moe couldn't pick up a signal, so hadn't managed to contact Finn. Kent had even worse news.

"I've got no fuel at all here. My main tank is in the boat, which is down at Mario's for a service, and my spare tank is empty."

Secret lagoon

It was time to make my first use of the Bocas Net for a situation which wasn't yet an emergency, but certainly had the potential to develop in that direction if Finn had had any problems. Using Kent's handheld radio I managed to contact Bruce, who was house-sitting for Bill and Janis.

"Please tell me you have some spare fuel there Bruce," I said.

"Yep, about twenty gallons. Where are you?"

Five minutes later Bruce arrived with a full can of fuel. With hurried thanks all round we filled our fuel tank, pumped the bulb, and fired up once again.

"Do you want to go looking for Finn first, or check at home to see if he's there?" I left the decision to Moe, knowing we only had about half an hour of daylight left. I was also worried the full tank of fuel probably only represented about half an hour of engine use. I really didn't want to run out in the dark, still not knowing where Finn was.

"Let's check at home first," she said, much to my relief. At least there we could pick up some more fuel too. "Do you think he will have made it by now?"

He certainly could have done if he hadn't got lost, but he'd only ever navigated the complicated entrance area to Dolphin Bay with us in a powerboat. It is pretty easy to get confused, particularly when moving slowly.

We all heaved a big sigh of relief to see the kayuko tied up at the dock. Finn had been back for a while, and had his feet up on the sofa, happily tucking in to an egg sandwich.

"Where have you lot been?" he asked. "I've been worried about you."

Big Red bites the dust

Gina arrived on the island in a sack, legs tied together with a piece of old string, looking a little distressed. She wasn't called Gina at the time. I never really had any intention of naming her, but she turned out to be such a character that I just couldn't help myself.

Juancho's brother Choppy, who was doing some work on the house for me at the time, brought her from his neighbour's farm. She cost me the princely sum of eight dollars.

"She a good egg layer," he promised me, justifying the price tag.

Gina proved to be a good egg layer within half an hour. We had untied her, leaving a reasonable length of string attached to one of her legs so she couldn't stray from the new hen house Choppy had just fabricated that morning, using leftover construction materials from the house. She had pottered around for a while, studying her new surroundings, then simply sat down on the ground and laid an egg. Choppy had secured his eight bucks.

"What is the Spanish word for a chicken like this?" I had asked Choppy. I knew that chicken ready to eat was called *pollo*, but understood that an egg-laying bird would have another name, similar to how, in English, *'cow'* refers to the living creature, *'beef'* the same animal served on a plate.

"This a *gallina*," he told me, pronouncing the double-l almost like a j.

"Gai-jina?" I asked. "Then she can be called Gina - she'll remind me of the Spanish word."

I kept Gina tied up on a long string for the first couple of days on Choppy's advice, until she came to accept the chicken coop as her new home. Each night I put her inside and closed the door.

When I finally let her off the leash she seemed to have settled. The first day she was loose she made me laugh out loud when she came hopping up the steps, wandered into the house, examined several nooks and crannies, and then made herself comfortable in the pantry. She sat there for a while. I was amazed when she got up and departed an hour later to find she had laid an egg there. Home delivery island-style!

This continued over the following days, a fresh egg delivered to my pantry each morning. Occasionally I would have it in the frying pan a couple of minutes after it was laid. You can't get eggs much fresher than that.

Big Red bites the dust

At first Gina proved to be a bit of a challenge at night. She had no desire to go into the luxuriously appointed hen house, and every evening I would have to go out to find her, perched in one of the trees near the house. I'd have to coax her out of the tree with a broom, and then shepherd her into the henhouse. If I left it too late she was very well camouflaged and difficult to find, but I wanted her locked inside, where she wouldn't fall prey to a raccoon in the night. When the builders had been working on the house construction they had told us they often saw a raccoon at night. They had trapped it one evening with a spring-loaded branch and some twine. The thing had wickedly sharp teeth, and was very feisty when we carefully released it the next morning. It would have no trouble polishing off Gina if it found her up a tree. However, it hadn't been seen since, perhaps scared away by its ordeal, but I didn't want to take any risks.

At one point I had to go away on what everyone in the archipelago referred to as a "visa run", as my six month visitor visa was about to expire. Many people, myself included, live in Panama simply as visitors, and all that is needed to renew the visa is 72 hours out of the country. Upon return a further six months is issued, as long as you have the required exit bus ticket or mocked-up travel itinerary. I left a good supply of chicken feed out, along with a big bowl of water, and Bill next door promised he would look in to see how Gina was doing as he passed by. I hoped she would manage on her own, knowing that leaving the henhouse unlocked at night for two nights was taking a bit of a risk.

When I returned I was pleased to she was fine, and I was amazed to find a little clutch of three eggs out on the back balcony. How on earth had she managed to lay them there? It took me a while to find out, and it wasn't until I had left the house doors closed one morning that I solved the mystery.

I heard a flapping of wings and realised that, unable to get into the house, Gina had taken an alternative route. She had flown up onto the balcony handrail. From there she had made a great leap onto the section of roof at the side of the house that supported the solar panels. She wandered along there, hopped up onto the half-wall surrounding the bathroom on the rear balcony, then down on to the balcony itself. With the back door being open on this occasion, she just wandered into the pantry and took up her usual laying position.

Choppy let one of his relatives know that I was looking for other chickens to add to my flock of one. A lady turned up in a powered kayuko at my dock one day with ten baby chicks in a sack. How many did I want? I took them all.

Paradise Delayed

I had no intention of naming these other chickens. Living on my own for six weeks, I managed to refrain from doing so. But with the arrival in mid-November of Moe and the kids, along with Australian friends Marty and Carol and their kids Bella and Maxie, the chicken naming began in earnest.

Gina was still queen of the roost, and out of the ten chickens that had arrived in the sack several months earlier, six were still with me. Four had not survived to meet the rest of the family. Two had died in infancy from what had looked like some sort of flu. I had segregated them to try to avoid illness spreading and both had died overnight.

The third death had been a bit of a mystery for a couple of days. There were originally four white chickens, of which one had died young. Whenever I went into town I would count the chickens on my return. They all roamed the island freely and I was vaguely concerned that the raccoon may return one day. On this occasion there were only two white ones pottering around. That evening, when I checked to see if they had all gone into the hen house before I closed the door, the third white bird was still missing.

It wasn't until a couple of days later that I found the dead body of the missing bird. It was in the inflatable freshwater pool which sits under the roof constructed for the solar panels. The poor creature had obviously hopped up onto the side of the pool and perhaps tried to drink some of the water. Once in, it would have been impossible for a waterlogged chicken to get back out over the rounded rim of the pool. I had to empty and clean the pool before using it again, as the water had a faint odour of decomposing chicken.

The final loss still remains a bit of a mystery. I inherited a dog from Ricardo, who had started doing some island clearing and crop maintenance work for me. He couldn't really afford to keep Campesino and offered him to me. My major concern was that he might polish off the chickens, but no, Ricardo assured me, Campesino had grown up with chickens around him all of his life.

Sure enough Campesino, which translates as *farmer* or *peasant*, paid little notice to the chickens, other than at feeding time, when his interest was more in the food than the birds eating it. The chickens soon got used to him. At the chaotic feeding time they would confidently run underneath the dog to get at some tasty scrap of food.

Occasionally the dog would take a half-hearted interest in the roosters, of which there were three at the time. He would follow them around, I think just for something to do. However, the more he did it, the more excitable

Big Red bites the dust

the roosters would get, flapping and crowing. The more fuss they made, the more Campesino wanted to follow them.

One morning I heard a huge flapping and fuss from the mangroves near the house. I looked out to see Campesino gazing out into the undergrowth towards the sea. The roosters were obviously in there and he had them cornered, which was causing a great deal of consternation among the birds. I scolded the dog and went down to pull him away, enabling the upset birds to return to the island. Unfortunately three had gone out and only two came back. One of the two handsome red roosters had gone AWOL and despite a thorough search, no sign of him was ever found.

I don't know if he just fell in off a mangrove root and drowned, or if perhaps a big barracuda had taken him. I'd seen a few largish ones swimming in the mangroves while snorkelling, but never anything that looked as if it could tackle a rooster. The poor bird was listed as missing in action, and his disappearance is now something of a cold case.

Maxie had a fascinating love-hate relationship with Big Red. The toiletry facilities at the house were still basic at best, being what I referred to as a "luxury bucket system". This basically meant that before the composting toilet was installed, the toilet was a plastic bag in a bucket, installed under a carefully cut and shaped piece of wood that supported a very comfortable toilet seat. There was a separate bucket filled with sawdust nearby. After use a small scoop of sawdust was put over the results of the visit to the facility. The whole system worked very well as long as the contents of the bucket remained dry. The obvious way to do this was to have everyone simply go outside somewhere to pee before tackling other matters.

Maxie was terrified of going down the stairs to use the "outside toilet", as Big Red, who almost the same height as her, would always be there, ready to chase her.

"Excuse me Ian," she would say politely. "I need to go out for a wee. Will you come down with me, 'cos Big Red knows you're the boss and he won't attack you?"

I had become Maxie's favourite protector, as Big Red never troubled me at all. I don't know if it was because he had known me when he was a small chick, if it was because I was the one who fed him and the others on a regular basis, or whether he just saw me as the big rooster, top of the pecking order. Whatever the reason, he never chased me at all, like all the others claimed he did them.

Paradise Delayed

I had tried to catch him in action, chasing any of the others, but hadn't seen any evidence of his crimes. Whenever I was there his behaviour was beyond reproach, yet I would regularly hear screams from below when I was upstairs, followed by complaints about his aggressive behaviour.

"Of course I will Maxie," I would answer, and we'd head downstairs where Big Red would behave impeccably. But upstairs ten minutes later Maxie would say that she needed to go to the toilet again, asking if I would accompany her.

This routine was repeated at regular intervals, usually until Carol interrupted, saying, "Give Ian a break Maxie. I'm sure you don't need to go for a fourth time in one hour."

She would assure us that she did need to go and we'd be off to face down Big Red again.

We had decided that it was time for one of the last two roosters to go. We hoped to breed from the remaining birds, and Big Red, being the most handsome of the remaining pair, was the obvious one to keep, at least as far as I was concerned. Turken, being the larger and uglier of the two, was the unfortunate recipient of the proverbial short straw, destined for the oven.

Friends Steve and Jeanne, one of the few younger couples in the area, both grew up in South Africa. While chatting with them about the noisy roosters one Sunday at Rana Azul, Jeanne told me, "I grew up on a farm. Killing a chicken? Yes, no problem. I'll be round this week to show you."

We had arranged to make dinner one day for a few neighbours. Steve and Jeanne arranged to come earlier to deal with Turken. I was a bit squeamish about the whole idea, as I've never really killed anything before. As far as I'm concerned, chicken comes wrapped in plastic from the deli counter.

Poor Turken was lulled into captivity by a small handful of food. In no time Jeanne had wrung his neck and had him laid out on the table set up for the grisly work ahead.

"Cut the head off," Jeanne told me casually. "It's dead now." The poor rooster looked anything but dead, thrashing about and flapping wildly, as I tried to cut through the neck. Jeanne had to step in and hold him again. She got a good dosing of blood from the neck, which I had failed to cut through cleanly, having been a little half-hearted with my first chop.

Big Red bites the dust

Steve stepped up and finished the job, also getting bloodied in the process.

"Maybe I'll just watch the rest of the butchery today," I suggested hopefully.

Jeanne dipped the now headless bird in a bucket of boiling water that we had prepared for the task and had the feathers stripped off in no time. Legs and wings came off, internals came out, and Turken now resembled something I would buy in the supermarket.

The next day, when we roasted him, Maxie was very quick to declare, "Mmm, Turken tastes good, doesn't he?" I think she was much less traumatised by the previous day's events than I had been.

Carol and Maxie continued to be Big Red's favourite targets, and we wondered if it was because they both had blonde hair. When they left to return to Australia things quietened down a bit, but then Moe and Maible started to complain about unwanted attention from the red rooster. Even Finn was scared of him. I often had to lead the way as we headed to the dock, ensuring the safety of all as we passed the ferocious bird.

He still behaved himself with me, and seemed to do so with the girls when I was around. I do think that most of the time he just followed people in the hope that they might be heading for the chicken food bucket, and the three terrified Canadians misinterpreted his intentions.

Of course with Turken gone the troublesome rooster was now firmly positioned at the top of the pecking order. Gina and the odd-looking brown egg-layer, who Moe had christened Whingdingdilly, regularly received his amorous attention.

The two remaining white birds were huge by now and it looked like it was time for them to be "processed". They were very heavy, and obviously had much more meat on them that even the huge Turken had had. I was mentally building myself up to the big day, steeling myself for the task ahead.

Ricardo was back doing some work at the property. As we sat chatting one lunch time, he pointed to a white chicken, saying something along the lines of, "She's going to be laying eggs very soon." At least this was my translation of what he said.

I fluently asked for further clarification, "Huh?"

He told me, I think, that when the red bits on the top of the head and under the chin - I have no idea what they are called - when these bits

Paradise Delayed

swell and turn redder, as they had done recently, they are about to lay eggs.

"Hoy o mañana," he told me. Today or tomorrow. Sure enough we got one egg that afternoon, and another from the other fat white bird the next day.

Beside my note saying "Kill 2x chickens" on my To Do list on the fridge I found Moe's message - "Save The White Ladies!!"

The Two White Ladies miraculously received a last minute stay of execution.

We were still collecting eggs from the other two females as well, but Whingdingdilly had started to become broody. I quickly built a smaller henhouse with two side-by-side compartments and we encouraged her to sit in one of the boxes.

We gathered her eggs, hopefully fertilised by Big Red, and added a couple of Gina's eggs too for good measure. With six eggs under her Whingdingdilly seemed content to sit all day.

With Whingdingdilly out of action Big Red only had Gina left. However, the White Ladies were now also in production, so he added them to his workload, enthusiastically going about his daily routine.

When Gina became broody too we put a handful of the white birds' eggs under her, and she sat in the box next door to Whingdingdilly.

Anticipation was high for the next three weeks, none of us quite believing that baby chickens would result from the eggs. Returning from Rana Azul late one Sunday evening Maible screamed with delight. "There's a baby chicken!!"

She had found it wandering about on the concrete floor, obviously having fallen out of the door of the small hatchery. We all crowded around the box as Maible carefully placed the tiny fluffy bundle back under Whingdingdilly, who carefully tucked it back underneath her own body. I put a piece of wood over the small open door to prevent any further escapes or misfortunes.

Over the next few days more eggs hatched and we all made regular visits to the chicken brooding house. Maible wafted around in a constant dreamy haze of utter happiness. I don't think she took in a word of her mother's school lessons that week, her mind simply filled with fluffy baby chicks. Sometimes she'd just sigh and say dreamily, "Oh, they're so cute."

Big Red bites the dust

The total survival rate was three babies for Whingdingdilly and four for Gina. Whingdingdilly had two brown babies, very obviously hers, and one yellowy orange one, which had to be Gina's offspring. Gina's four babies were all white, all from the White Ladies. With any luck we'd have a couple of good egg layers from the first three and four bigger birds for the oven.

Maible, however, didn't want to hear any talk of ovens, having promptly named each chicken as it arrived.

The next Sunday at Rana Azul we chatted to our near neighbours Bill and Janis. Maible told them at great length about the chickens, what each was called and why.

Janis laughed, as the lady who occasionally cleaned her house was related to Choppy. She was the same lady who had delivered ten chickens to me in a bag. Janis told me that she had been chatting to Garmina about me one day.

"Is dat de man who name him chickens?" Garmina had asked. Oh dear. It appeared that I was getting a bit of a reputation as a slightly eccentric gringo. Maible's chicken naming was only serving to enhance the reputation. However, I don't imagine I'm the only gringo here considered to be eccentric by the locals.

Moe and the kids had been pestering me for some time about killing off Big Red. I had been postponing the inevitable day, not wanting to do the deed. Despite his early morning crowing, which then continued throughout the day, I quite liked him. I was also very entertained by the fear he instilled in the other three, while never once putting a scaly foot wrong with me.

I had used the fact that we needed a male bird to end up with fertilised eggs as a reason to prolong his stay of execution, but once the seven babies were born that reason became null and void. I still wasn't really very enthusiastic about killing him.

However, one day, as I walked underneath the house, Big Red didn't step aside as he usually did. He squared up to me, jumping up and flaring his feet forward. He had obviously decided that with Turken out of the way, now was the time to make his challenge for ultimate supremacy of the island. I was having none of it and gave him a good punt with my foot. "I'm the big rooster around here," I laughed. I couldn't fault him for trying, but I decided not to tell the others.

Paradise Delayed

A day later, as I was leaning over to peer into the hatching coop to check on the baby chickens, I felt a hefty whack on the back of my legs. I turned around to find Big Red glaring at me in what looked like a very defiant manner. He obviously hadn't learned his lesson from the previous day and was setting himself up to have another go at me. I grabbed the nearest thing to hand, which was a decent piece of wood from the scrap lumber pile. Like a cricketer facing a tricky bouncing ball, I played a blocking stroke as the rooster jumped at me again. We sized each other up once more and I swung my makeshift bat back, planning to knock him for six, to continue the cricketing analogy. I didn't hit him with full force, but I was determined to knock the fight out of him. He looked a little taken aback. Before I got the chance to deal another blow his nerve left him and he turned and fled, with me in hot pursuit.

He was too fast for me so I gave up the chase and stormed up the stairs. "Right. Today's the day. Where's the big knife? We're doing in Big Red."

"He attacked you, didn't he?" Moe asked, unable to hide her smirk.

"No. Well, maybe.... okay, yes, he did. His time has come."

Moe and the kids were keen to help. Moe came downstairs quickly with a very sharp knife, keen to follow through while I was obviously committed to the deed. All we had to do now was catch him. I tried wandering up to him casually, but still mindful of the clattering he had just received, he didn't seem to want me anywhere near him. He kept running away whenever I approached him.

I suggested one of the others should grab him, but the fearful trio didn't want anything to do with the big bird until he was securely trussed up. Okay, I thought, food. The chickens always come at the slightest rattling of the food bucket lid, so I opened the container and spread a small handful of grain. The other chickens gathered around my feet and started clearing up the grain, while Big Red approached but kept just out of arms length. I threw a little more food in his direction, hoping to entice him closer, but he pecked at the grain with one eye still watching me carefully. When I tried to grab him he skittered off sharply.

"What now?" I asked Moe and the kids. From the shed Moe produced a large piece of netting that had been laid around since Cameron had looked after the place. I had no idea why he had it or where it had come from, but it could serve well to catch the wary rooster.

In a scene that may have looked like something out of Gladiator Moe and I stretched the net tight while the kids tried to wrangle Big Red in our

Big Red bites the dust

direction. When we pounced the wily bird somehow slipped out from the closing trap and put some distance between us and himself.

I'd had enough by now, my anger wearing off, replaced by amusement at the ridiculous carry on. "I'm giving up for now. I'll catch him unawares at feeding time tomorrow morning," I suggested. "I'm going to have a shower."

Moe was not so easily deterred and ten minutes later I turned around in the shower to see an amazing spectacle. She had found another net, this time one on a pole - the type that is used to scoop a big fish up out of the water when caught on a fishing line. She had it held high above her head and was running across the island like some demented butterfly collector. "Go on Moe!" I shouted encouragingly, almost helpless with laughter at the scene. Big Red was running fast, but Moe was determined and gaining ground on him slowly. It was as exciting as any close-run Olympic race, but the result was inevitable - Moe was not going to be beaten by a bird.

Poor Big Red looked sad trussed up in the net. Even Moe felt sorry for him, but we were committed to our course of action. I steeled myself and twisted his neck as Jeanne had demonstrated so competently with Turken. He died quickly and, I hope, reasonably painlessly.

It didn't take long to strip his corpse of feathers after dipping the body in a bucket of very hot water, but neither Moe nor I really had much idea about gutting and cleaning the carcass. It took quite a while and much discussion before we finally had a bird that looked ready for the oven. I resolved to find out more about the butchering process before trying again.

"Alright, we're gonna butcher a chicken," drawled Russ, in what I believe is an American Deep South accent. "I'm surprised everyone doesn't know how to do this, so we thought we'd make a little how-to video..." he continued.

After the comical debacle with Big Red, I had gone directly to the fount of all knowledge - YouTube. I searched for info on the proper way to kill and butcher a chicken and in particular, the removal of the innards.

I had discovered "Survival Skills With Russ - How to butcher a chicken", which had a wealth of five star reviews. Russ is a no-nonsense kind of guy. In no time has the chicken strung up, throat slit, stripped of feathers and innards removed. Eight minutes - job done. Easy!

Paradise Delayed

The next morning was D-Day for the Two White Ladies, who were ridiculously easy to catch compared to the Big Red Wild Goose Chase of the previous week. The merest tapping of the food bucket lid brought them running enthusiastically to their doom.

Once again, I still felt a little queasy at the neck breaking part. I had to wear some thick gloves so as to distance myself from the deed slightly, but steeled myself and did it quickly.

When killed and stripped of feathers Moe and I took one each. Following Russ's advice we had the insides pulled out in no time. The two birds looked as fat and plump as anything out of a supermarket fridge. We were very proud of our handiwork.

Having lived free-range on the island since they were chicks, the two birds were as organically raised as possible and I don't think I've ever had a tastier chicken dinner.

Even Maible commented on how tasty and tender the meat was, but she still didn't want to hear about the baby ones growing up to ultimately face the same fate. I felt none of the remorse over eating the White Ladies that I had when Big Red was served up, as they had been a little characterless and dumb. Big Red had had personality, even if it had been a somewhat annoying one.

He used to start crowing around 5am, and would then continue to crow throughout the day at irregular intervals. He had been an ever-present part of life on the island, and I was going to miss him - just a little bit.

RIP Big Red.

Jungle wedding fever

Anticipation was high. It was the first wedding that Rana Azul had ever hosted, and two members of our little community were getting married. Joseph and Maria had pulled out all of the stops and the place looked spectacular. Michael greeted us at the dock, a stiff whiskey already clutched in his slightly shaking hand.

We had come down with Bill and Janis. It was wonderful to have them back home after such a long absence, while they had spent some time in the States. Everyone had been looking forward to today, which was something a little bit out of the ordinary - a change to the usual round of social gatherings and the regular Sunday outing to Rana Azul.

Marianne arrived on schedule, despite Michael's vague concerns that she may not. The ceremony was simple and heartfelt, conducted by one of our little community, Wayne. Few people had had any idea that he was a fully ordained minister.

For me that is one of the beauties of living in the lagoon. Everybody has the choice to share as much or as little of their past as they wish, and can make a completely new start among new friends. People here tend to take each other at face value, accepting each other as the people they are right here, right now.

The meal was delicious and, as always, I was impressed by the quality of the offerings from our hosts, who each week manage to produce a wide and varied menu in such a remote location. The champagne flowed, as did plenty of other drinks, and the tables were cleared away to create a dance floor for the remainder of the daylight.

After the couple's first wedding dance Moe and I got up for a couple of songs and then Maible insisted I join her to whirl her around the dance floor for a while. As the afternoon progressed I chatted with many of the other guests. As I often do on a Sunday afternoon, I found myself sitting with Steve and Jeanne, the "youngsters" house-sitting a lovely property in the next bay.

Our friendship had grown over the year or so we had known each other. I always enjoyed their company, as we shared many similar interests.

Jeanne was having a great time, and pointed out many of the dancers out on the floor. A few of them were regular dancers on a Sunday afternoon, but the little area was jam-packed today with people who generally didn't tend to get up to dance.

Paradise Delayed

"Oh, this is such a scene. Look at them all. There has never been such excitement here." It really was quite a sight to see so many people from an older generation, so obviously enjoying their golden years.

"It's Jungle Wedding Fever," she exclaimed, and I burst out laughing. That's exactly what it was.

Twenty or thirty years from now, I thought to myself, as my own twilight years approach, I hope I will be up on some dance floor somewhere, enjoying my own version of Jungle Wedding Fever.

Epilogue

When I arrived in Whitehorse, in the warm summery weather of July 2010, I knew that my stay there might be short-lived. It was an ideal place to settle for a while to write my first book, *A Life Sold*, but once that was published in November, I found myself with a lot more spare time on my hands.

As winter deepened and temperatures plummeted towards minus 30 degrees (Celsius, that is - about minus 22 Fahrenheit!) I decided it was time to head south. Little did I know that I was to become the owner of a Caribbean island within six short months.

But I have always lived life in a somewhat one-day-to-the-next fashion. In *A Life Sold* I wrote at some length about my belief that life is meant to be an adventure, and that we all only have a short span allotted to us. I just want to squeeze as much experience into my time as possible.

Buying a Caribbean island has certainly added to the collection of experiences and adventures that have filled my life to this point. But it hasn't all been about my own experiences. As I found on my two year goal achieving adventure, the journey became less about the goals, and much more about the people I met along the way.

Living in Bocas del Toro has been the same. What has made life here an absolute delight is not simply the place, the weather, the lifestyle or the creatures - it's the people.

There is such a wonderfully eclectic group of interesting characters here. By its very nature I think Bocas attracts people who think a little differently, who want something more out of life, and who are prepared to take action to achieve their dreams.

The atmosphere at Rana Azul on a busy Sunday afternoon is amazing. It is, by far, my favourite part of the week. I feel like I am part of a big family and I am grateful to the wonderful people here for welcoming me into their little community.

Everyone here could write a book similar to this, filled with tales of challenges overcome, dangers faced and comedic encounters. They have all experienced the same steep learning curve, and have scrambled successfully to the top.

I often think back to my conversation with Kitty when I first arrived in Bocas. My suggestion of a *Caribbean Island Life for Dummies* handbook had been rejected, and I now fully understand what she meant. Everyone

Paradise Delayed

here has earned the right to be here. It makes them the fascinating and entertaining group of people I have come to know and love.

But - there is always a "but", isn't there? - maybe now it's time to look for my next adventure. While I am very happy here, I'm not quite ready for the retired life, and neither am I much of a grower of crops. I've overcome all of the big challenges - the island is clear and some crops are already growing well, the house is built and is very comfortable, and I hope not to sink any more boats - no guarantees there though. I can only sit on the porch reading books for so long before the need for some action starts to gnaw at me a little.

There are still so many things I would like to do and so many places I still want to see. It's a big world, I have a long list, and I'm not getting any younger. Time to move on, I think.

However Bocas, and in particular the people here, will always have a very special place in my heart. I'll be back often to visit, I promise.

Ian Usher

April 2013

Note: For book extras, including photos illustrating each chapter, and some video clips too, please go to:-
www.ParadiseDelayed.com

Acknowledgements

I've said it before and I don't hesitate to say it again - the most vital ingredients of this amazing adventure are the people I have met in Bocas del Toro. Without the help and support of so many I would have been "lost in the mangroves" for much longer.

From our first arrival in town Mark at Beyond Bocas Realty was of great assistance, and has since become a great friend. In the early days of island clearing and planning, advice from Eric and colleagues Robert and Stefan was invaluable. Thanks to Andy at Hotel Las Brisas for putting up with my boat, tools, chainsaw issues, workers, and endless questions.

My island clearing team were wonderful to work with, and included Fernando, Otis, Napoleon and Roman. Juancho and brothers Choppy, Raoul, Boy, and the rest of the team constructed a comfortable and solid home for us.

My wonderful first nearest neighbours, Bill and Janis, became almost like jungle parents to me, and I couldn't have managed what I did without their help, support, and the loan of a boat every now and then.

Kent and Marcie superseded Bill and Janis as my nearest neighbours when they started building in between us, and have since become great friends. I will always be grateful to them for being so understanding about my clumsy ways, especially with their lovely big boat.

Cameron did a great job of house-sitting for three months. Thrown in very much at the deep end, he adapted quickly and soon became a much-loved member of the community.

Captain Ron took me under his wing and insisted that I take an active role in the Bocas Net, both as controller and weather reporter. The net is such a vital part in the widespread community, and he, Captain Ray and others do a wonderful job in keeping it friendly, fun and informative.

Bill and Janis introduced me to Bruce, who fixed the second-hand propane fridge I bought and only requested payment in cold beers when the fridge proved its worth. Since then Bruce has been a near neighbour while house-sitting Bill and Janis's place, and happily took over looking after our place when we headed for Canada once more.

Brent and Jan were supporters from early on, and Brent's advice, along with Captain Ron's, on solar panels was invaluable. I'm glad you made me listen and get a bigger system than I had originally planned.

Paradise Delayed

Steve and Jeanne offered a somewhat younger outlook than many of the residents in the bays, and had actually heard of most of the music I like. They have become great friends too.

There are so many others that make life in Panama so much fun. Among those are Mary and Carl, Chocolate Dave and Linda, Lyn, Peter and Jane, Wayne and Linda, Rick, Sherry and Elle, Cathy and Laurie, and many others.

Cynde's lovely house has been the focal point for many social gatherings, and she is the best hostess. Hank and Linda lent me a monster tile cutting machine, which halved the trauma of tiling bathroom, living room and kitchen counters.

Horse Dave and Molly are always fun to be around. Dave's horse trek through the jungle to the local village is a must-do activity for all.

Johne and Aeon have been good friends to the kids, giving them an experience of a lifetime at the helm of the beautiful *Second Star*. They have also been good friends to Moe and I too. Many other sailors have also been great companions as they have breezed through, as was Sam, who house-sat the beautiful Casa Kayuko resort, and looked after us so well when we were there.

Almost last, but by no means least, at the absolute social centre of my Bocas-based life are Joseph and Maria, and their wonderful restaurant Rana Azul. It's so much more than just a restaurant, and I can't imagine Bocas without you guys there.

Finally, my hugest thanks to Moe, Finn and Maible for being my co-adventurers on this part of the journey. It wouldn't be any fun without you.

Thanks to Moe also for her tireless editing work.

Oh, and thanks of course also to those who've made the journey to come and visit: Peter, Craig and Gemma, Martin and Rachel, Sean and Heather, Marty, Carol, Bella and Maxie, and Stan, Alia, Elias and Taiya.

Apologies if I have missed anyone - if you feel you should have been mentioned here, then you should. The oversight is mine and I apologise profusely - I'll rectify the fault in the next edit of the book - there are bound to be a few typos I've missed.

About the author

Ian Usher was born in 1963 in Darlington in the north-east of England. He grew up in the small northern market town of Barnard Castle, and went to college in Liverpool, gaining a teaching degree in Outdoor Education.

A varied and chaotic career followed, involving many jobs, locations and businesses. From 1992 to 1996 he ran Scarborough Jet Skiing in partnership with long-time best friend Bruce.

He moved to Australia in 2002 with his wife Laura, but following a painful separation in 2006, Ian put his life up for sale on eBay in 2008 as the final step of the process of moving on.

Two years of travel followed, in which he tackled a list of 100 goals, aiming to achieve them all in a period of 100 weeks. The whole amazing adventure is chronicled in the book "A Life Sold", and the movie rights to the story have been purchased by Walt Disney Pictures.

Ian settled for a while in Canada with Moe, and her children Finn and Maible, but a wandering spirit and a severe winter resulted in the search for a warmer lifestyle. The result of that search was the purchase of a small Caribbean island, and the adventures related in this book.

* * * * *

There are more photos illustrating the stories in this book, online at:-
www.ParadiseDelayed.com

Further background, including blogs, photos,
videos and more at these sites:-

www.ALife4Sale.com
www.100goals100weeks.com
www.IanUsher.com
www.MoeBoksa.com
www.CaribbeanLife4Sale.com

Published by:
www.WiderVisionPublishing.com

* * * * *

Also by Ian Usher, available in both paperback and digital format:-

"A Life Sold"
What ever happened to that guy who sold his whole life on eBay?

A LIFE SOLD

What ever happened to that guy who sold his whole life... ...on eBay?

by
Ian Usher

What on earth would make someone decide to put their whole life up for sale... on eBay?

When Ian Usher decided that it was time to leave the past behind and move on to the next chapter of his life, that is exactly what he did. The results were surprising, entertaining and challenging.

However, the auction was only the beginning of the adventure. What does someone do when they have sold their life? Well, just about anything they like really!

Armed with a list of 100 lifetime goals, and a self-imposed timeframe of 100 weeks, Ian embarked on what could truly be described as the journey of a lifetime – a global adventure spanning six continents, two years, and almost every emotion.

From the amazing highs of achievement, happiness and love, to the terrible lows of disappointment, loneliness and despair, come along and enjoy the rollercoaster ride of life, as experienced by one traveller who is simply looking for a new start.

Further details at:-
www.ALifeSold.com

CPSIA information can be obtained at www.ICGtesting.com
Printed in the USA
LVOW062006260413

331153LV00001B/169/P